SOCIAL USAGE

SECOND EDITION

SOCIAL USAGE

ANNE R. FREE, *formerly of*
The Pennsylvania State University

Prentice-Hall, Inc., Englewood Cliffs, New Jersey

Printed in the United States of America

ISBN: 0-13-819607-9

Library of Congress Catalog Card Number: 69-11706

10 9 8 7 6 5 4 3 2

PICTURE CREDITS:

INVITATIONS AND NAME CARDS: *Tiffany & Co.* and *B. Altman & Co.*, New York.

PHOTOGRAPHS OF TABLE SETTINGS: p. 106, from the November 1967 issue of *McCall's*, photographed by Paul Dome; p. 112, top, *Den Permanente*, Copenhagen, Denmark; bottom, designed by Ray Wills of *Georg Jensen, Inc.*, with accessories compliments of *Georg Jensen, Inc.*, New York, and photographed by Charles E. Andrews.

PRENTICE-HALL INTERNATIONAL, INC., *London*
PRENTICE-HALL OF AUSTRALIA, PTY. LTD., *Sydney*
PRENTICE-HALL OF CANADA, LTD., *Toronto*
PRENTICE-HALL OF INDIA PRIVATE LIMITED, *New Delhi*
PRENTICE-HALL OF JAPAN, INC., *Tokyo*

Preface

The author first became aware of the need for a compact book on modern social usage when she was invited to teach this subject at The Pennsylvania State University in 1947. Since then over 25,000 students in all majors, both men and women, have elected to take this course. Students and others have asked more than 200,000 questions on etiquette—clearly indicating the extent of the young person's need for help in this area. Students want to know not only what is expected of them on campus but what will be expected of them when they leave college. These questions and talks with groups on and off campus point up contemporary social usage problems.

This book was written at the request of these many students and others. The author hopes that it will help in solving the daily problems we all encounter and that the simple but vital information given here will aid all who read the book to experience more rewarding social and business contacts.

The author wishes to thank Mrs. Willis Parker for her valuable suggestions and assistance in the preparation of the manuscript, and Maria Erdelyi, of Appleton-Century-Crofts, who illustrated correct and incorrect table manners in the photographs on pages 98–103. She wants also to express gratitude for her husband's encouragement and deep interest in the book.

A. R. F.

Contents

*There is no accomplishment so
easy to acquire as politeness, and
none more profitable.*

—G. B. Shaw

I

What Is Social Usage?

We all have manners. They may be good manners, bad manners, or indifferent manners, but we cannot avoid having them. This is because human beings are a *social* and not a solitary form of life. In order for us to survive, we must be together and we must interact with each other. Our manners are our mode of interacting.

Kipling's little wild boy, Mowgli, had manners—the manners of the wolf-pack, but after he had his first bruising contact with his own kind, he said, "They have no manners, these men-folk." The fact that Mowgli was a charming and impossible fiction does not alter the point here—that the manners of wolves and of men differ. Manners differ among different groups of men, too, and over many hundreds of years widely varying "codes of etiquette" have developed throughout the world. The *etiquette* of any society is its accepted code of good and bad manners. Etiquette is more than this, but this is its fundamental meaning.

Social usage is based on manners and includes etiquette. It is possible for a person to have good manners—kind, considerate, polite manners—without knowing anything about etiquette. Social usage is largely determined by environment—where we live, in what period of history, and under what economic and social pressures. Environmental conditions, as they change, cause human behavior to change,

1

but this usually occurs very slowly. When the mode of living changes, the rules of etiquette that no longer apply are discarded. Every generation discards rules that no longer serve a useful purpose and develops new rules to fit new conditions. The deciding factors in adopting such new rules should be: do they serve a clear and obvious need? will they simplify living? are they in good taste?

Environment and our human and personal heritage *determine* who and what we are. Who and what we are determines how we act, what our behavior patterns are; this brings us full-circle back to social usage and accepted custom. The term *social usage* refers to the routines, conventions, etiquette (all modified by courtesy and the exercise of good taste and consideration for others) to which we conform in order to have harmonious relations with other people.

Lacking conventions, individuals batter against each other like rocks in a landslide. Knowing the conventions, we slip into the grooves effortlessly and flow along smoothly with our fellows. When the grooves become too deep and seem to be inescapable, however, we tend to lose touch with reality and mistake conventions for human character. This is why the idea of etiquette long ago fell into disrepute in the very real world of the American frontier. "Good manners" we Americans have always respected, but perhaps more than any other people in history we have resented and rejected "false manners."

The word and the idea of etiquette has found its way back into respectable usage, however, in most of our society, as American behavior-patterns have matured and won world recognition. We use the word *etiquette* in this book as the French originally used it. *Etiquette* in French means *ticket*. In the gilded days of the great French kings a ticket was a card upon which directions and rules, or notes, were written. *Tickets* of instruction and proper court behavior were presented to people who were to make an appearance at the royal court. *Etiquette* thus became the rule, the guide to correct (acceptable) behavior in a social situation.

As we use the term, a *social situation* exists whenever two or more individuals are reacting to each other. This may be a face-to-face occasion or it may be communication by telephone, by letter, or in any other way. Etiquette provides us with the code for specific social situations in much the same way as rule-books provide us with rules for tennis, football, and other games. If we know the rules well, we play the game better and enjoy it more.

Knowing the rules is only part of the answer, however. As we said above, etiquette must be exercised with courtesy, good taste, and consideration for others.

Courtesy combines two very important ideas: _kindness_ and _politeness_. An unkind act is never a courteous act, no matter how "correct" it may be. An impolite act cannot be a courteous act, and it is difficult to imagine an impolite act that is "correct."

Courtesy is . . .

. . . consideration of others in little things.

. . . thoughtfulness.

. . . the friendly voice.

. . . the phrase "thank you" when said with sincerity.

. . . true democracy in relations with all other persons.

. . . the ready respect for and encouragement of attainments beyond one's own.

Courtesy is _not_ . . .

. . . behavior that deliberately irritates others.

. . . late-to-keep-appointments behavior.

. . . "stampede" behavior—pushing ahead of others.

. . . unclean, scenery-spoiling, rubbish-scattering behavior.

Courtesy, when it has become an instinctive part of a person's behavior—when it seems to have been inborn, most effectively supports etiquette. Courtesy will become "instinctive" in all of us if we consistently and intentionally foster courteous behavior in every social situation.

The opposites of courtesy are rudeness and thoughtlessness, and these are greater hindrances to good human relationships than the breaking of any specific rules of etiquette. A person who knows the rules thoroughly need never hesitate to break them if following them dogmatically will hurt someone else. The point is, we must not break the rules through _ignorance_.

Ignorance of the civil law is not considered an excuse for breaking the law. Does ignorance excuse an individual who breaks the rules of etiquette? The answer is, not very often! There are two kinds of ignorance. A person may be ignorant of the rules—of what is right and what is wrong. This kind of ignorance can be cured by instruction. Such a person is unintentionally ignorant and is willing to learn. The other kind of ignorance is deliberate ignorance. The deliberately ignorant person is the one who thinks wrong doesn't matter. This person should be avoided in both the business and social worlds. The great fault concerning ignorance lies in not trying to cure it when the opportunity presents itself. The best time for teaching the fundamentals of etiquette, like the fundamentals of democracy, honesty, and thoughtfulness, is in childhood and early youth, but we keep learning all our lives, and what we have not learned in childhood we can learn as adults.

Good taste, like courtesy, is essential to good social usage, and ignorance of it is not an acceptable excuse. What do we mean when we say that such and such an action, or costume, or conversation is or is not "in good taste"? The phrase comes originally from the way things taste to us in our mouths. From this we apply the concept of taste to our intellectual and esthetic appreciations. Good taste is concerned with the fitness or suitability of things. It suggests the ability to recognize good proportions, orderliness, symmetry, and beauty. By extension it implies a "feel" for the incongruous, the ugly, the unkind, and the unsuitable in human relationships.

Social usage, etiquette, courtesy, and *good taste* are the four key terms that will appear in this book. They have been described and defined in the preceding paragraphs and will occur many times in the following chapters. One point remains to be made here, and that is the importance of *studying* social usage as a means of improving one's ability to get along with other people.

Getting along with others is an art that we can acquire, and it is one of the most important areas of our education. Feeling secure in our human relationships, we are relieved of embarrassment and can experience a fine and deep enjoyment of life. Whatever our age or occupation, getting along with others is vital to us. Knowing the conventions of acceptable behavior is fundamental. In business, school, and other *work* situations, tact, patience, and recognition of the rights and privileges of others are essential parts of the code. This is equally true of our *social* lives if we are to rub shoulders with each other without friction. Observing the mechanical conventions is like pouring oil on the moving parts of an engine. It lubricates and allows the engine to work.

This book is going to describe the mechanical conventions and accepted behavior patterns as they appear in the etiquette of the present time. Where local customs differ from those suggested here, the reader must weigh these differences in the light of the basic meanings of good social usage before deciding for or against the particular custom. Our aim here is to make available the knowledge of widely accepted patterns. In following these patterns the individual will most of the time and in most places be in harmony with other people.

A TEST ON SOCIAL USAGE

The following statements are concerned with certain fundamentals of social usage in ordinary daily life. Several possible patterns of behavior are suggested in the phrases that complete each statement. If you select the most-acceptable-behavior phrase automatically, accurately, and with self-assurance, you have social poise and are probably at ease in most social situations. If you have to search for the correct phrase, however, you are probably unsure of yourself. Further study of social usage and the simple rules of etiquette will be of great help to you and will contribute to your harmonious relationship with others.

This is a phrase-selecting, self-administered test, which you can take at your leisure and mark in any way you wish. There is no "answer sheet," but each statement is accompanied by a page reference indicating where each of these behavior problems is discussed. Check (in your book or on a separate sheet of paper) the phrase which you believe most suitable. Then turn to the indicated page and verify your decision.

1. A man offers his hand when being introduced   (page 21)
    a. to an older woman.
    b. to a young woman.
    c. to all men and women.
    d. to all men.

2. When eating soup one should   (page 82)
    a. never tip the bowl.
    b. tip the bowl away from you.
    c. tip the bowl toward you.

3. If an intimate friend is asked at the last minute to fill a
    place at dinner,   (page 132)

   a. he should accept if possible.
   b. he need not accept because of the late invitation.
   c. he should regret, politely, knowing the hostess is wrong
      to ask him at such a late date.

4. You have been a weekend guest at a friend's home. To
   show your appreciation,   (pages 161–162)
   a. a printed thank-you card with your signature should
      be sent.
   b. a note and gift should be sent as soon as you return
      home.
   c. a note must be sent; a hostess gift is optional.

5. All formal invitations and their acceptances or regrets are
   written in   (page 139)
   a. the first person.
   b. the second person.
   c. the third person.

6. A married woman has her name card engraved   (page 154)
   a. Mrs. Mary Jane Briggs.
   b. Mrs. Walter George Briggs, Jr.
   c. Mrs. W. G. Briggs, Jr.

7. When passing your plate for seconds, you should   (page 96)
   a. put your knife and fork completely on your bread-and-
      butter plate.
   b. balance the used tips of your knife and fork on the
      bread-and-butter plate.
   c. leave your knife and fork on your dinner plate.
   d. hold your knife and fork in your hand to avoid having
      them fall from the plate in passing.

8. John received a wedding announcement from a former
   college friend. It is necessary that he   (page 149)
   a. write an acknowledgment.
   b. send a gift.
   c. It is unnecessary that he do anything.

9. A husband with his wife signs the register in a small motel
   thus: (page 220)
   a. Mr. and Mrs. John Smith.
   b. Mr. John Smith and wife.
   c. John Smith and Nancy Smith.
   d. John Smith and wife.

10. When she is dining out, a woman may correctly place her
    purse   (page 53)
    a. on her lap.
    b. on the table.
    c. on the floor.

11. When a death has occurred and you wish to express your
    sympathy to the family, you should   (page 164)
    a. call them on the telephone and say how sorry you are.
    b. send them a printed sympathy card with your signature
       on it.
    c. send them a very brief handwritten note expressing
       your sympathy.

12. When a husband and wife attend a dinner party together,
    they are seated   (page 53)
    a. directly across the table from each other.
    b. separately, not directly opposite each other and not next
       to each other.
    c. together, with the husband to the left of his wife.

13. During a business interview, the initiative in offering ciga-
    rettes is taken by   (page 203)
    a. the interviewer.
    b. the person being interviewed.

14. Silverware which is not clean may be wiped off with your
    napkin   (page 67)
    a. at a friend's house.
    b. under no circumstances.
    c. in a restaurant.
    d. anywhere that it seems necessary.

15. One acknowledges introductions with   (page 20)
    a. "Pleased to meet you."
    b. "I am glad to make your acquaintance."
    c. "How do you do."

16. A taxi driver in a city is tipped   (page 228)
    a. nothing if the fare is under $.60.
    b. nothing unless the driver helps with the luggage.
    c. 20 per cent on fares over $.60.

17. A friend of the bridegroom who has never met the bride
    sends his gift to   (page 192)

    a. the groom only.
    b. the bride only.
    c. both bride and groom.

18. At a party the hostess shakes hands with   (page 21)
    a. all guests, men and women.
    b. only the women.
    c. only those who offer to shake hands.

19. In introducing two of his acquaintances to each other, a man should say   (page 15)
    a. "Ralph Scott, this is my friend Bob Turner."
    b. "Ralph, this is Bob."
    c. "Ralph Scott, this is Bob Turner."

20. In an *American Plan* hotel the rates usually include   (page 221)
    a. room only.
    b. room with breakfast.
    c. room and two meals.

21. A man's name card to be used for commencement announcements should read   (page 153)
    a. John H. Adams.
    b. Mr. John Henry Adams.
    c. John Henry Adams.
    d. Mr. J. H. Adams.

22. You have been invited to dinner and an unexpected guest arrives to visit you. You should call the hostess who has invited you to dinner and   (page 124)
    a. ask to bring the guest.
    b. explain the situation, then regretfully decline the invitation.
    c. give your regrets without mentioning the guest.

23. The person who first rises from the dinner table at the end of the meal is   (page 69)
    a. the guest of honor.
    b. the hostess.
    c. the host.

24. A goblet is held by   (page 97)
    a. grasping the stem.
    b. holding it near the top.
    c. holding it midway, with fingers on both top of stem and bottom of bowl.

25. When an airline hostess gives you extra attention because you are ill, you should, when you leave the plane, (page 223)
    a. thank her only.
    b. tip her and thank her.
    c. tip her only.

2

These passengers, by reason of their clinging to a mast, Upon a desert island were eventually cast. They hunted for their meals, as Alexander Selkirk used, But they couldn't chat together— they had not been introduced.

—W. S. GILBERT

Introductions

There is more than a caricature of English polite society in the quotation that opens this chapter. There is a clue to the meaning and prominence of the introduction as a social maneuver of great importance. Human personalities, like sovereign nations, are separate entities, and, we like to think, are inviolable. Theoretically we can be required to make the acquaintance of another individual only by our own choice. We are strangers? We may pass each other with indifference on the street. Once an introduction has taken place, however, we can never be completely indifferent to each other again. Society has one code for strangers and another for acquaintances. The introduction bridges the two. It may lead to the most casual—the so-called nodding—relationship, or it may lead to a close friendship. In either event, it initiates a social situation of significance.

An introduction smoothly accomplished allows the newly introduced participants to concentrate on each other. An introduction awkwardly accomplished embarrasses everyone concerned and spotlights the introducer, to the detriment of the new relationship. The socially relaxed person is almost always competent and automatically correct in the introduction situation. His friends are at ease with him, knowing he can pilot them adeptly into new relationships. His is a skill worth learning, and, like all of the social accomplishments, it can be learned only through study and practice.

10

As with other social patterns, it is important to remember at the outset that introduction patterns differ with cultural background. Eskimos of some tribes greet each other by rubbing noses. Frenchmen, and other Europeans, not infrequently show pleasure in an introduction by a cheek-to-cheek embrace. In the United States we are sometimes more rudely indifferent than are people of many other cultures. Such misconceptions and errors may result from ignorance, or they may suggest a fear of character softness that goes back to our frontier roots.

It is true that social finesse was a factor of little positive value in the uncrowded world of the frontier, but in the close-contact civilization of today it approaches the dimensions of a necessity. We cannot avoid daily, hourly, contacts with our fellows. We cannot afford to give each new contact unlimited time or energy for development. Social patterns—grooves—make the courteous routines easy and habitual. We follow them as we follow the rules of a game, and the better we are at the play, the more satisfying will be our rewards.

Let us consider the code as it relates to introductions. We will summarize, below, a number of commonly accepted practices. Reading and memorizing these, however, will not put us at ease in the introduction situation. Only practice will accomplish this. We must practice at every opportunity until introductions come with as much ease as the putting on of shoes. If we must stop to think of correct order or form, we lose confidence and poise. Should opportunities for practice in daily life not be adequate, we can persuade family or friends to practice with us. Barring this possibility, we can try a return to childhood make-believe. A room to oneself is all that is needed. A mirror is a useful prop. Play-act every conceivable situation. The results will be well worthwhile.

Introductions Should Be Friendly

"Politeness is to do and say the kindest thing in the kindest way." Formality does not preclude warmth, kindness, consideration. Remember the following suggestions when you are the introducer or the introduced.

1. Smile. If you do not appear to enjoy these people, you can hardly be honest in expecting them to enjoy you or each other.

2. Look at the person to whom you are speaking. This may require you to make a quick shift from the person you have introduced to the one you are about to introduce, but it is vital to success. Most of us have had the embarrassing experience of greeting the wrong person in a tightly packed social situation because of a darting-eyed friend whose mind was not on the introduction he or she was conducting.

3. Be sure you know the names of the persons you are introducing before you launch into the act. The "I-remember-your-face-but-I-can't-remember-your-name" routine is sourly familiar to most of us. We are lucky if we have not participated in this on both giving and receiving ends. The recommended procedure is, Think before you act! If you wish to introduce these people and do not remember one or both names, try to approach them privately and refresh your memory before getting them together. If you find yourself catapulted into the situation, however, you may beg to be forgiven for your unreliable memory. In this situation it is probably better to forget both names than to remember one name and forget the other. When you have made the introduction situation an instinctive part of your social reaction, this distressing occurrence will not often plague you.

4. Speak distinctly and keep your voice and manner unhurried. The curt nod, hurried handclasp, and perfunctory repetition of a phrase have no place in good human relations. This is the brush-off and is a low point in bad manners.

5. Repeat the name of the person to whom you have been introduced. This is not a social requisite, but it is friendly and it is a great memory-booster. If you repeat the name again when you part from your new acquaintance, this will augment the pattern and you will have a good chance of remembering both name and face when you meet again. Say, "How do you do, Mr. Adams," and later, "Goodbye, Mr. Adams," or "I am very glad to have met you, Mr. Adams."

Remembering names is a tremendous asset in both social and business life. People like to be remembered, and to be remembered correctly. This builds good will and is an effort that may enhance your own interest in other people—an obvious benefit to your personality.

6. Include a conversational lead in your introduction. This gives the new relationship something to build on. Say, "John Smith—

Lester Baxter"; then to John, "Lester too is interested in photography." Or say, "Mrs. Gray, this is Mrs. Jones. I believe both of you ladies have summer cottages on Cape Cod."

7. Practice an acceptable style until it has become second nature to you. Then forget about yourself and concentrate on putting other people at ease.

To Introduce—or Not to Introduce

The rule of kindness and comfort in the social situation prevails. Never err on the side of caution here. When in doubt, go through with the introduction. Better a social mistake than an insulted friend.

In general, introductions are in order whenever two or more strangers are together in company with a mutual friend. The mutual friend, obviously, is master or mistress of ceremonies in this situation.

Make sure that friends visiting in your home are made acquainted with members of your family who happen to be at home at the time. Conversely, never neglect to introduce your parents or older members of your household to your friends.

At a chaperoned party or dance, introduce your partner to the chaperons. Should the affair be a very large one, it is adequate to make the introductions to several chaperons with whom you are acquainted.

Guests at parties must always be introduced, either to each member of the group if the party is small or to several other guests of congenial outlook if the party is large.

Teas, at-homes, cocktail parties are often held with the express purpose of acquainting people of similar interests. The introduction is therefore an inherent element in such a party. The host and hostess and designated friends do their best to see that all guests are introduced. In the often noisy disorganization of such a gathering, however, guests may often find themselves on their own, and in these circumstances they are expected to introduce themselves and to find common topics for conversation with other individuals or groups. Upon leaving such a party, incoming and outgoing guests may nod in friendly fashion to each other but need not stop at this point for introductions.

Introductions should NOT take place under circumstances which disrupt some group occupation or interfere with an intimate conversation. Neither are they necessary on the street or in such public places as the theater lobby or a restaurant when making the introduction will be physically awkward or when it is likely to be an annoying interruption for one of the individuals involved. Thus, a group at dinner in a restaurant is not required to stop eating and greet the acquaintance of one of its members when the acquaintance pauses briefly to chat on his way to another table. A group walking together on the street does not wait to be introduced if one member drops back for a moment to greet an acquaintance who happens to walk by. The group moves on slowly until their other member rejoins them.

The Words We Use and How We Arrange Them

The modern introduction is the historical outgrowth of the *presentation* once practiced only in the courts and salons of kings and nobility. In many ways today we ordinary citizens live like kings and queens, and, much simplified, many courtly mannerisms and attitudes have become customary with us.

Thinking of the introduction as a presentation, we realize that the introducer is in fact presenting one individual to another individual. Who receives the presentation and who is presented? Following the rule of courtesy, consideration, and due respect, and barring complicating circumstances which we will take up later, we always *show deference to* (that is, *present to*) ladies; older individuals; high-ranking dignitaries in the church, government, military services.

In uncomplicated social situations, any of the following forms are good:

Mrs. Worthington—Mr. Adams.

Mrs. Worthington, *do you know* Mr. Adams? (or *you have met* Mr. Adams, *haven't you?* or *have you met* Mr. Adams?)

Mrs. Worthington, *may I introduce* Mr. Adams? (or *I should like to introduce* Mr. Adams; or *may I present;* or *I should like to present.*)

Mrs. Worthington, *I should like you to meet* Mr. Adams.

Mrs. Worthington, *this is* Mr. Adams.

Mr. Adams, *I should like to introduce you to* Mrs. Worthington.

If deference is being shown to age, the forms would run, "Mr. Sixty—Mr. Thirty"; or "Mr. Sixty, do you know Mr. Thirty?"; and so on. If deference is being shown to rank, the form is "Bishop Hall —Mr. Sixty" and so on. If deference is being shown to eminence, use the eminent one's publicly known name and follow the usual forms: "Mrs. Roosevelt—Mrs. Sixty."

Should your tongue slip and you find yourself deferring to the wrong individual, don't apologize. This is not a crushing social error. Try to introduce these individuals to others of your acquaintance later, and do it correctly. They will overlook the first incident. Or you may be able to recover sufficiently to use the last of the forms above: "Mr. Adams, I should like to introduce you to Mrs. Worthington."

Should you, perchance, find yourself introducing your mother to the President of France, you say, "President Blanc, may I present my mother?" Or you use any other of the acceptable forms. Heads of states and other persons of very great eminence are always deferred to over everyone else present, regardless of age, sex, or any other special condition.

SOME WORDS AND GESTURES THAT WILL NOT DO

1. Never *command* people to meet each other.
   Never say, "Mrs. Gray, meet Joe Brown."
   Never say, "Jack Gray, shake hands with Joe Brown."
   Never say, "Jack Gray, meet the wife."

2. It is usually safer not to use the word *friend* in making introductions. "Mrs. Gray, this is my friend Miss Brown," may give Mrs. Gray that "shut-out" feeling. She would like Miss Brown to know that she, Mrs. Gray, is also your friend. In introducing your friends to your family, however, this caution is unnecessary. It is very good form to say, "Mother, this is my friend Joe Brown."

3. Do not repeat names unnecessarily. It is awkward as well as poor form to say, "Mrs. Black—Mrs. Smith; Mrs. Smith—Mrs. Black."

4. Gesturing with your hands while making an introduction is usually not advisable. If done gracefully, and with polish, it may lend charm to the situation. More often, however, using the hands is a cover-up for social inadequacy, in which case it appears awkward. Never, of course, do you point to the person being introduced. Pointing is always in extremely bad taste.

NAMES AND TITLES IN THE INTRODUCTION

First names. It is common usage in many groups today to use first names and skip the *Mr., Mrs.,* or *Miss.*

Betty Smith—John Stout.

Caution should be observed, however. In introducing youth to age, or anyone to the really elderly, it is probably wise to retain titles.

Miss Eighteen—Mr. Fifty.

Mrs. Eighty—Mrs. Fifty.

Strangers and young people do well to let older and better-known persons take the lead in first-naming. A noticeably younger person does not call an older one by first name unless asked to do so, even if the older person has been introduced with first name and no title.

In the business situation, custom sometimes dictates full name use in introductions. Do not, however, use first names until you are familiar with your new role. That you are introduced as John Jones does not indicate your status to your co-workers. You may be on the executive level or you may lunch with the office boy. It may simply indicate that you are just one more member of the big happy family. Nor does a first-name introduction indicate their status to you. It may seem stuffy to say Mr., Mrs., or Miss, when you are introduced to Bill or Mary, but familiarity can come later, after you have found out where you stand.

Titles. Mr., Mrs., and Miss are of course nearly always good form when used in introductions. However, there are occasions when other titles, or no titles at all, are preferable.

Use the *medical* title *Doctor* at all times when introducing a medical doctor or dentist. A woman doctor is often referred to socially as Mrs. or Miss. Try to learn her preference before you are confronted with the problem of introducing her. If in doubt, introduce her as Doctor.

Use the *academic* title *Doctor* at all times for college and professional people properly so called, unless they specifically reject this form. This is particularly important in the business and industrial world. In the academic world the title is less important for prestige but perhaps more important as a convenience.

Socially, many Ph.D's ask to be introduced as Mr., Mrs., or Miss. Obey such a request. The following are good form:

Dr. Brown, this is Dr. West. Dr. West is a chemist with the XYZ Corporation.

Then to Dr. West you add,

Dr. Brown is a medical man here in Centerville.

When introducing *couples* with titles, you may say,

Dr. and Mrs. West—Mr. and Mrs. Gibson.

Then you immediately add,

Mrs. West is Dr. Ruth Greene.

Or you may introduce this couple by saying,

Dr. David West and Dr. Ruth West, may I introduce Mr. and Mrs. Gibson.

If only the wife has a title, you may say,

Mr. West and Dr. Ruth West, this is Mr. and Mrs. Gibson.

Other academic and official titles—*President, Dean, Professor*—may be substituted for Doctor and are preferred usage for most campus affairs. The student says,

Mother, may I introduce Professor Brown.

Dean West (dean of women), I should like to introduce my room-mate, Mary Smith.

Protestant clergy are introduced as *Mr.*, unless they hold advanced degrees, in which case they are introduced in the same way as are academic doctors. No clergyman is ever properly introduced as Reverend. This is a grammatical and social error. Reverend is an adjective. It is not a title. The Reverend Albert Joyce is introduced to our friends as Mr. Joyce or as Dr. Joyce.

Catholic priests are always introduced as *Father*, never as Mr. or as Reverend.

Jewish clergy are introduced as Rabbi, or, if they hold advanced degrees, as Doctor.

Members of religious orders may usually be introduced as *Sister*, or as *Brother*. However, it is well to check on this in advance whenever that is possible.

Such Church titles as *Canon, Dean, Bishop,* and of course *Monsignor, Cardinal, Archbishop,* supersede the title of Doctor and usually supersede Father. Preferred form of introduction varies in different churches. You will do well to consult your church functionaries if you are likely to face the problem of introducing such dignitaries.

Introducing Relatives and Oneself

In introducing relatives, special problems may arise. It is easy to fall into pomposity or excessive formality here. It is also easy to lapse into uncomfortable informality. Your young sister is not "Miss Smith" and she is not "Meet the kid!" She is "My sister Jane." The following suggestions may be helpful:

1. Omit the surname whenever it will obviously be the same as your own.

Mother, this is Bill Owens.

Miss Russell, may I introduce my father?

2. If your sister, Jane Smith, is married to Joe Brown, you introduce her as "My sister, Jane Brown."

3. The term *mother-in-law* is good usage, as is *step-mother* and *step-father*. Surnames are usually needed here, as they may differ from your own.

> Mrs. Biggs, I should like to introduce my mother-in-law, Mrs. Robertson.

> My step-father, Mr. Drum—Mr. Black.

4. Husbands and wives not infrequently find it necessary to introduce each other. Socially a man introduces his wife as "Jane" or as "my wife." A woman introduces her husband as "John" or as "my husband." In business only will they use Mr. Green or Mrs. Green.

> Mr. Hall, I should like to introduce you to my wife.—*Social*

> Mrs. Brown, have you met Mr. Green?—*Business*

In introducing oneself, first names are generally approved usage. However, where the age or position difference is considerable, more formality should be observed.

> I am Joe Abbott, your new neighbor across the street.

> I am Mrs. Harvey, your mother's girlhood friend from Illinois.

> I am J. P. Harvey (or just Harvey) of Centerville, Illinois, an old friend of your father's.

It is quite proper to introduce yourself to other guests at any party where you find yourself alone, and a stranger. This can happen at college or church affairs as well as at large private parties where the host or hostess cannot be constantly at your side. Also, always introduce yourself to members of the faculty at college social functions.

> Mr. Jaspers, I am John Brown in your Tuesday art class.

Introduce yourself to others having interests in common with you at resorts, on long trips, or under almost any circumstances where the reason for your interest cannot be misunderstood. Do not go around introducing yourself to celebrities, however. Use common sense and good taste here, as in other social relationships.

HOW TO ACKNOWLEDGE AN INTRODUCTION

A successfully accomplished introduction depends upon both the introducer and the introduced. The people being introduced, however, have a comparatively easy time. They may respond to the introduction acceptably with any of the following phrases:

1. "How do you do." This is the all-purpose response. It is good at any age and in all circumstances.

2. "I am very glad to meet you." This must be said with sincerity to carry conviction and is suited to the warm and out-going personality. Used by other people it may sound stilted and over-formal.

3. "I am delighted to meet you" is good when the occasion justifies this degree of enthusiasm. Age handles this phrase more naturally than does youth.

4. "Hello," followed by a first name, belongs to youth. Just *Hello*, with no name, is abrupt. Say, "Hello, Jane," or "Hello, Bob."

Some phrases in rather common use have a jarring impact and get the introduction off to a bad start. Try to *avoid saying:*

1. "Charmed," or "Delighted."

2. "Pleased to meet you." This is lazy and is likely to sound like "Pleez t'mee'tcha."

3. "I am pleased to make your acquaintance." This is awkward, icy, and incorrect. Don't use it.

4. "How are you?" This is a question where no answer is desired. It embarrasses the person it is directed to and should not be used.

5. "It's a pleasure."

6. "Howdy."

THE HANDCLASP AND THE ACT OF RISING

The handclasp. This is a gesture of trust. Men holding weapons cannot shake hands—not if they are right-handed! Although this is hardly a problem today, to our ancestors it was a matter of life and death. The handshake survives as a "must" expression of friendliness in our Western culture.

Men *always* shake hands upon being introduced to each other unless some physical impediment prevents this—a dining table in a crowded restaurant, for instance.

Men remove gloves for the handshake whenever this is at all possible (another gesture of trust—"no hidden weapons here!"). Exception: if gloves are used with formal dress they are not removed to shake hands with either men or women. They are part of the costume.

Women may shake hands when being introduced if they wish to do so. English women nearly always shake hands. American women often prefer the friendly smile and nod.

Younger women wait for the older woman to indicate whether she wishes to shake hands.

If a man is being introduced to a woman, it is the woman's place to proffer her hand or not as she chooses.

Women *do not* remove gloves for the handshake.

Both host and hostess *always* shake hands when greeting guests.

A guest when leaving makes every effort to shake hands with the host and hostess.

If a receiving line is involved, guests always "go down the line" shaking hands with each individual there.

Always be alert to a proffered hand. There are few humiliations more painful than that of having an extended hand rejected or ignored.

Make your handclasp a good one—not limp and not viselike. A friendly handshake builds good will. Look at the other person and smile when you extend your hand.

When to rise. The act of rising is another guesture of respect, of deferring to a person whom one holds in high regard. The familiar principles apply here. Men defer to women. Youth defers to age. All defer to eminence. We can list the customs briefly:

Men *always* rise for introductions, whether to another man or to a woman.

Except as noted below, women *do not* rise for introductions.

Young women should rise for older women if the age difference is considerable. For instance, Miss Twenty-one should rise for Mrs. Fifty, but Mrs. Forty will retain her seat when she is introduced to Mrs. Fifty.

Both host and hostess rise to greet their guests, and again when their guests are taking leave.

Both men and women customarily rise when being introduced to a member of the *clergy*.

Both men and women rise when being introduced, or when introducing themselves, to a prospective employer.

Both men and women rise when being introduced to persons of *eminence*. A woman's judgment must be employed here. Only she can decide whether the eminence is sufficient to command her deference. If she should be the only woman to remain seated, however, this would be in very bad taste. She should rise if all others rise.

GROUP INTRODUCTIONS

These are to be avoided whenever possible. Few people have memories that will retain a rapid listing of new names. However, sometimes such an introduction is unavoidable. It will help if you observe the following suggestions:

1. Repeat the name of the person you are introducing only once. Then name the other individuals in the room in the order in which they are seated, or standing.

2. If practicable, take the person you are introducing to each new acquaintance separately, allowing the usual handclasp and personal greeting. In this situation, as in the one above, you need mention the name of the person being introduced only when he or she first enters the room.

HOW TO TAKE LEAVE

"Dwelling on good-byes," as one writer has said, "is useless. It is not the being together that it prolongs, it is the parting."

Good form always dictates a brief leave-taking. There are several convenient and suitable ways to say good-by. The following expressions will see you over the threshold or will advance you from one social situation to the next at a large party.

You may say, "I am very glad to have met you," or "I have enjoyed meeting you," or "I hope to see you again," or combine these expressions if you wish. As you speak you will be shaking hands or nodding and smiling a farewell, then turn away.

The other person will reply, "Thank you, and I am very glad to have met you," or "I, too, have enjoyed meeting you," or "I shall be very happy to see you again," at the same time accepting your hand-clasp or returning your farewell nod and smile.

The simple word _good-by_ is often adequate for leave-taking, particularly among young people. It will sound friendlier if followed by a repetition of first names and by smiling.

3

Conversation

Words, spoken in conversation or written on paper, were to Jonathan Swift the tools of his craft. How well or ill he handled them determined the quality—and quantity—of the roast he was privileged to carve. Most of us do not experience so direct a dependence upon words for our immediate well-being. And yet words are one of the primary facts of social relationship. Our fellow humans can see us. They can feel us. And they can hear us, and they know that we can hear them. Talking—the use of words—is as normal in the human being as is walking or eating. Through talking we communicate our ideas and our needs. But talking is not what Swift meant, or what we mean, by conversation. When Ogden Nash wrote that he'd traveled in five foreign countries without trouble, although all he knew of the languages were the two words *please* and *thank you*, he was providing a valuable example of the universality and usefulness of good manners, but he would have been the last to call this communication conversation.

Conversation is the intelligent exchange of ideas through the use of speech, whereas *communication* can take place without speech, if necessary—by means of a gesture, a noise, a look. Longfellow, who said, "He speaketh not and yet there lies, a conversation in his eyes," might more accurately, if less poetically, have written "communication in his eyes." We have all been recipients of the meaningful look

24

and know it can be a poignant experience, but it is a lean substitute for the conversational give and take which is the mainstay of our social relationships.

Little children experience no difficulty in conducting their conversations. They are direct, open, and uninhibited. Neither grammar nor social taboos impede the movement of a thought from the baby mind to the baby tongue. But the complexity of living soon changes this. With maturing consciousness of self all too often comes painful self-consciousness, and this is nowhere more painful than in the area of conversation.

Children go to school already able to talk. They must learn to talk grammatically. They must learn that there are times to talk and times not to talk; that to some people they may talk in one fashion and to other people they must talk in another fashion; that there are some subjects about which a child does not talk, and other subjects about which he must talk whether he wishes to do so or not. From a conversational point of view it is possible to suspect that the whole period of our childhood is one long series of traumatic experiences, and the wonder is that we reach maturity with any remaining impetus toward conversation. The strength of our need for this social relating is implied by the fact that we do indeed continue to have a very strong impetus toward conversation. Nevertheless, we often reach high school or college age with our conversational abilities in a state of psychological and sociological confusion. What can we do to relieve embarrassments and to unblock our friendly impulses?

Our first need is to understand the elements that are involved in conversation. These are

First, *the human voice*, which has *quality* that, within limits, can be controlled.

Second, *speech*—the use of words to convey meaning—which, to be socially acceptable, must be *grammatical*.

Third, *intelligibility*, which involves *pronunciation* and *enunciation*—characteristics that allow your conversational partners to understand what you are saying.

Fourth, *ideas*—something to talk about—which implies *intelligence* and *knowledge*.

Fifth, *suitability-awareness*, which requires perception of the cultural pattern of taboos and liberties—the *etiquette* of conversation.

THE HUMAN VOICE

Musicians regard the human voice as a musical instrument having range, depth, resonance, tone. Like manufactured instruments—the violin, for example—it can by its sound alone arouse emotion in the listener. It can also be trained and altered through practice and growth to produce desirable change. It is this characteristic that makes it unnecessary for anyone to have, or at least to keep, an unpleasant, harsh, shrill, or coarse-grained voice.

How does your voice sound to other people? Until recent times, man was never able to hear his own voice as others heard it. In this age of recording devices, however, nearly all of us have had this experience. It is a very valuable experience and worth going to some trouble to obtain if one's school life or work life has not included it.

In this book we are concerned primarily with the effect of your voice in the social situation.

Is your voice loud? We call it ear-splitting and nerve-racking. We invite you only to our noisiest parties. We are careful where we go in your company. You attract embarrassing attention.

Is your voice weak? We suspect you of being a timid personality. You irritate us because we have to strain to hear you. We invite you only to our smallest and quietest occasions. You are helpless in a gay gathering.

Is your voice high and sweet (or shrill)? We may ask you to sing high soprano for our entertainment, but if you maintain this voice in conversation we suspect you of insincerity. You make our nerves jump. Listen to the continuous playing of a fife or the Scottish bagpipes for confirmation of this effect.

Is your voice harsh and aggressive? We suspect you, as well as your voice, of being dictatorial, impatient, nervous. You put us on the defensive. We are more ready for a fight than for a friendly conversation.

Is your voice nasal? We suspect you of having adenoids and wish you would see your doctor. We cannot listen to *what* you say for distress at *how* you are saying it. Monotony sets in and we escape your company as soon as possible.

What then are the qualities of a pleasing voice, a "good" voice? A pleasing voice is *well-modulated* but not artificial; it is *low* (within your voice range) but it is not weak; it is *expressive* but it is neither shrill nor aggressive. A pleasing voice is a confident, controlled voice. It is, by its *quality*, able to command and to hold attention.

Few people achieve such a voice without some conscious effort to do so. Listen to your own voice on a recorder. Ask others how your voice sounds to them. You can probably correct your own shortcomings, or if your problems are great, seek professional help through a speech clinic or voice teacher.

SPEECH AND GRAMMAR

This second of our conversational requirements could take us probing into the vast and fascinating area of the linguistic sciences and arts, an area far beyond the scope of this book. Here we are concerned with the fact that for our social living we need words, and in using words we need to know "what is to be preferred and what avoided, in the inflections and the syntax of (our) language." (From the definition of *grammar* in *The Merriam—Webster Dictionary*.) We need, that is, to be able to use our words grammatically.

Grammatical speech is not hard to acquire. It is in common use and our personal weaknesses are corrected from infancy by parents, teachers, friends. The danger lies in carelessness and, more often, perhaps, in obtuseness and obstinacy—refusal to see or admit the grating effect that distortions have on the listener.

Speech, barring physical impediments, we all have. Good grammar we may have at will. Vocabulary, wealth in our word supply for conversational needs, we acquire only with effort and use. This means, in effect, that we acquire vocabulary as we increase the range and depth of our interests and relationships. We may, by rote, learn the meaning of the word *viscosity*, but it will not serve us in conversation and will soon be forgotten unless we are in a social situation in which viscous substances are under discussion. The deliberate effort to increase vocabulary is always valuable, however. It rouses curiosity and stimulates alertness, with obvious advantage to conversational ability.

INTELLIGIBILITY

Our voice quality and the grammatical use of words are of little conversational value if our listener cannot understand what we are saying. Good pronunciation and careful enunciation are to our conversation somewhat as grooming is to appearance. They are an evidence of our own self-respect as well as of consideration for the listener. Such childish and slovenly impatiences as "I gotta go now" or "wanna-come-a-long?" or any of a long list of similar offenses often last far into adulthood without correction. They are fatal to mature conversation. Listen to your own voice *and* to your own pronunciation. Force yourself to slow down, to pronounce every syllable. Work to correct the faults that only you can change.

Localisms, regional accents, dialects, are frequently looked upon with pride and perpetuated by people who take their geographic origins very seriously. Nevertheless, they greatly increase the problem of intelligibility in conversation. If a native of the state of Georgia talks so that only another Georgian can understand him, then he will be at great conversational disadvantage outside the boundaries of Georgia. This is the age of radio, television, the recording instruments, and of travel. Especially the young travel the length and breadth of the country and of the world. Their parents and teachers and they themselves should make certain that localisms in speech do not raise unnecessary barriers.

IDEAS

Conversation cannot take place in a mental vacuum. To converse, we must know something to converse about, and we must find a subject of mutual knowledge and interest with our fellow conversationalist. Good conversation is a reflection of the things we see, hear, read, feel, or otherwise have learned. So-called born conversationalists, to whom the knack of ready speech seems to come naturally and easily, have groomed themselves—unknowingly, perhaps —for this role. The good conversationalist has a lively, versatile mind and a liking for people. Conversely, those of us who like other people and who have a broad range of interests are likely to be good conversationalists. This is a skill which responds to use and training. By cultivating diverse interests and keeping alert to our surroundings and to matters of current interest we may usually have something to contribute to a conversation, even though it is not in the area of our special interests.

The idea content of a conversation is heavily dependent upon the social situation that brings it about. Young people at a dance are unlikely to get into deep philosophical or political discussions; ladies at an afternoon tea are likely to talk community affairs, fashion news, personal experiences of themselves and others; a group of professors around a dinner table will surely find themselves conversing in depth in one or more of the many fields of interest they represent. At a cocktail party, we may say that the field is wide open—discussion may remain on the lightest plane or it may assume profound seriousness.

No matter what the social situation is, however, conversation must concern itself with subjects about which the participants know something. Hence, the more extensive your knowledge, the greater your opportunity to take part in this satisfying relationship.

SUITABILITY-AWARENESS

This is the fifth of the conversational elements we are to consider and the one with which we are most concerned in this book. The remainder of this chapter will be devoted to some guidance in the many aspects of what is really the *etiquette* of conversation.

We have already suggested that to be able to talk well is a tremendous asset and that there are few attainments that give greater satisfaction in our contacts with other people. Our way of saying things—voice, pronunciation, grammar—has much to do with the success we achieve in putting our ideas across and even in making friends. The impression of sincerity in conversation is pleasing and can be cultivated. It must, of course, be sustained by real personality sincerity to be of lasting value. A relaxed, well-adjusted person talks easily and seldom has conversational problems of any great seriousness. Most of us, however, probably make some of the common mistakes or have a few of the common difficulties, especially in the area of conversational manners. The following "conversational guide" may be of help in calling attention to special problems.

A CONVERSATIONAL GUIDE

Are you a chatterer? Do you fear silence? Some people fear a speech vacuum as much as they fear pain. Such people may be temperamentally nervous, psychologically taut, or they may simply have developed the habit of chattering. They are usually ill at ease in the social situation, and they will carry on a one-sided conversation to the death if no one rescues them. Perhaps they are hobbyriders and discuss some interest of their own at great length without discovering anything about their listener. They become known as bores, and their acquaintances avoid them. They are voluble, but in fact they fear the conversational situation. The cure for this condition, like the cure for most fears, lies deeper than the symptom, and a psychologist could be of much help. However, if you know yourself to be a chatterer, it may be worth your while to attempt to analyze your own problem. Try imposing deliberate silences on yourself. You may find that you like the results.

Are you a good listener?—or do you always seize the conversational reins? The English essayist Richard Steele once said, "When you fall into a man's conversation, the first thing you should consider is whether he has a greater inclination to hear you, or that you should hear him." If you do this, you will not find yourself sometime explaining to a new acquaintance the fundamentals of the planned menu only to learn later that you have been talking to a graduate dietitian. There is an art in listening. A good listener learns that a well-timed phrase or an encouraging query may keep an interesting talking companion going for a long time. Absent-minded listening is rude. In general, the good listener *appears* interested because he *is* interested both in what he is hearing and in the person who is speaking. A good listener contributes to a conversation quite as much as does the good talker.

Are you a man (or woman) of silence? This is not the same as being a good listener. The man of silence is often a person who would very much like to talk but who has not been able to unlock the psychological floodgates. He consoles himself that he only speaks when he has something worthwhile to contribute to the conversation. He is seldom a good listener, because he is not at ease, and he is not interested in what is being said or in the people who are saying it. He is not a social success. Such a person may undertake a program of deliberately forcing himself to take part in a conversation. If he weathers the awkward beginnings of such a program, he may in time discover that it is possible to direct a conversation into areas of his own interest and knowledge. In other words, he can become a good conversationalist.

Can you handle small-talk? Small-talk is perhaps the lowest form of conversation, but it is like salt in the soup—we can't do without it. Casual meetings of friends on the street; the conversation following the introduction of strangers; social situations of superficial character—we need a reservoir of words and sentences to fit these occasions. It is difficult for many people to talk with strangers. It is difficult for some people to chat over the teacups. What can be done to relieve such embarrassments?

Actually, there is no excuse for lack of conversational topics except mental paralysis. Conversation is give and take, and the person finding himself at a loss in a small-talk situation may start things moving by being the first to give. That is, tell your new acquaintance something about yourself first. Tell him, perhaps, where you live, what you do, or mention an amusing event involving yourself, some member of your family, your dog or cat. Usually, your new acquaintance will be eager to exchange information of this sort. You each question the other casually and without probing. You find that you like similar sports, or TV shows, or that you or your children have similar school problems, or that you have read the same books. You may be at the start of a fine friendship or you may be "ships that pass in the night," but with the great majority of people you must go through this introductory small-talk before you can get into the deeper waters of big-talk conversation. Use the light approach for these occasions and keep your deep insights for a more suitable time and place. ". . . Beautiful words," says Longinus, "are in very truth the peculiar light of thought, (but) . . . stately language is not to be used everywhere." Stately language has no place in small-talk. Be casual. Be friendly. But *talk*.

Are you a name-forgetter? We have discussed this fault in connection with the making of introductions (see page 12), but it occurs frequently enough to warrant its being mentioned again here. Never embarrass a recent acquaintance or an old friend by starting a conversation with, "You don't know who I am, do you?" Better by far, if there is a chance that you will not be recognized, to start with this assumption and say immediately, "How do you do, Mrs. Ward. I am Bob Smith." Then give Mrs. Ward some clue as to where you have met by saying, "That was a wonderful party Jack Allen gave, wasn't it?"

Or if you yourself are the chronic forgetter of names and the other person is not alert to your problem, it is usually best to make a quick confession of your ignorance and hope to have some plausible excuse handy. Then proceed with your conversation; perhaps your friendliness may overcome the unhappy fact of your poor memory.

Are you considerate of others in your conversation? Very rarely will people deliberately injure others in their conversation. Nearly all unkindnesses are spoken thoughtlessly. But words are powerful weapons for promoting prejudices, quarrels, misunderstandings. Words are also the barbed instruments of flattery, that, "like base coin, . . . impoverishes those who receive it." Words can both rouse and express emotion, and ill-conceived conversations have many times corrupted friendship. The brutally frank person *may* be on psychologically sound ground, but he should be aware that this is also very dangerous ground. His "helpfulness" may be misconstrued.

Are you a hesitant talker? Do you talk in gulps and indulge in long pauses while you fish for the exact phrase, the precise memory? Somewhere on the conversational plateau there is doubtless an ideal level where ideas, words, and time come into perfect balance. Most of us tend to grab the first word that comes to mind which happens to fit our need—or, we try the patience of our listeners by a series of halting sentences and tortured probings of the memory or of our vocabulary reserves.

If we are of this latter habit (which has its virtues as well as its faults), we are likely to develop speech mannerisms or other mannerisms to fill in the painful pauses. We may hold grimly to our control of the conversation with *uh* (or *ur*)—*uh*—*uh*—*uh*, or, lost in thought, we may habitually pull at our lower lip, or our ear, or hunch our shoulders spasmodically, or polish our glasses, or if we are at table we may shred the paper napkin, or keep wiping up real or imaginary crumbs, or we may polish the wooden table with our hands. We are most certainly not relaxed. These habits are often annoying to watch, but few of us are completely free of them and we need to exercise charity in condemning them in others. We can, however, make every effort to avoid them in ourselves.

> Once more; speak clearly if you speak at all;
> Carve every word before you let it fall.
>   . . .
> And when you stick on conversation's burrs,
> Don't strew your pathway with those dreadful *urs*.
>   —O. W. HOLMES

TABOOS IN CONVERSATION

Be wary of the personal question. Tact and a sensitivity to your companions' feelings are essential here. "Questioning is not the mode of conversation among gentlemen," said Samuel Johnson. Some people seem never to achieve this understanding. The following reminders suggest some areas into which it is bad form to pry.

1. DON'T ask a person's age, or weight, or dress or suit size. Women will resent this and many men regard it as "none of your business."

2. DON'T ask a person's religion, or politics, or national origin, or race. If you desire to discuss these things, first tell your companion *your own* status, and if he or she wishes to fall in with your lead, the topic is then open.

3. DON'T ask "financial" questions. You may be dying to know how much Helen paid for her dress, her home, her furniture. You may wish you could compare notes with Dick on his insurance, his inheritance from Uncle Bob, his taxes. And *you may learn all these things* by leading the conversation in such a direction, but never by the direct question method. Costs that are public knowledge, as of a refrigerator or other appliance, school tuition, commutation rates on train or bus, are more open to direct questioning, but even here sensitiveness to the kind of person you are talking with should influence you.

4. DON'T ask for details about your friend's illness, or family troubles, or job troubles. Your friend will volunteer these readily enough if he or she wishes to talk about them. Avoid making your own troubles a conversational crutch. This can be just as boring in you as in your friends.

5. DON'T ask about physical or other handicaps. Handicapped persons are often sensitive to an extreme. They are also often help-less in some area of normal activity. The matter-of-fact approach is to be recommended. Offer to help when help is needed but otherwise ignore the situation. Your blind or paralyzed friend is generally quite normal mentally and has normal interests. He is frequently a good conversationalist. If the handicap is a speech or voice impedi-ment (such as extreme stuttering), this will require more finesse on your part. The rule of "ignore" is still good in so far as it is at all possible. If your contact with such a person is frequent, you will be wise to consult his family or teachers or close friends as to the most useful response. How you handle these conversational problems, whether you are aware of it or not, is a part of the therapy which may improve or worsen the handicapped person's condition.

Be wary of the use of slang and strong language. Slang, collo-quialisms, coined words and phrases, add color and expressiveness to your conversation and, carefully used, they have value. The Eliza-bethans, Shakespeare among them, coined words lavishly and the English language throve on the results. Unless you are making lan-guages and grammar your special study, however, guard your speech from too much slang, or at some crucial moment, you may find your-self unable to distinguish good usage from the unacceptable. Slang is exceedingly habit-forming. It is a lazy way of talking, and in many conversational situations it is both inappropriate and offensive.

Be wary of the following conversational bungles:

1. DON'T boast—of successful relatives, of celebrities you have met, of yourself or your possessions. This is childish and embarrasses your listeners. If compliments are given you, however, respond with a simple thank-you. Protesting a compliment is like asking for more of the same. You enjoy it so much you want to keep the subject going.

2. DON'T pretend to know something you do not know. Time and fate will surely find you out. If you have a smattering of knowl-

edge in some area, let your listener know that you are interested, but that your understanding of the subject is superficial.

3. DON'T be afraid to say, "I don't know." This is a mark of sincerity which is respected even though you may be teased a little for some void in your arsenal of learning. It is also an invitation to conversation on that subject, and you may learn something.

4. DON'T monopolize the conversation. Stories about your children, your pets, your bridge or golf game, are useful small-talk and are not to be neglected, but they must not be overdone. One or two anecdotes can be amusing and enlivening, but don't hold your listeners to this line for the entire conversation.

5. DON'T repeat your stories. If you are a successful teller of "good ones" that you heard somewhere, keep your reserve of tales constantly changing. You can be a valued addition to the conversational situation, but you must be alert to the deadly nature of repetition. "What horrors," wrote Oliver Wendell Holmes in his *Autocrat at the Breakfast Table*, "when it flashed over him that he had made this fine speech, word for word, twice over!" The teller of tales at a party is in the role of dramatic entertainer, and he must study his audience. Long stories must be told with careful pacing and control or they will be dramatic fiascos. It is especially painful to have these repeated to the same audience.

6. DON'T say, "I've heard that before," if the conversation brings out stories or jokes you are familiar with. You spoil the fun for the other listeners and embarrass the talker. Your contribution is negative and probably rude as well. If you are in the presence of a confirmed "repeater of stories," learn how to head him off by getting control of the conversation yourself and starting it in some other direction.

7. DON'T interrupt.

8. DON'T contradict. If you disagree, do so pleasantly and without arousing bitterness and hostility. Suggest that there may be another way of looking at this thing. Don't say bluntly, "You're wrong!" You are likely to bring the conversation to an abrupt halt. This is especially true in the areas of religion and politics. Keep the discussion intelligent, lively, but unemotional.

9. DON'T indulge in unpleasant mannerisms while speaking or listening. This includes drumming on the table with your fingers, gesticulating, wetting your lips constantly, pushing your face close

to your companion's or withdrawing it jerkily as if your friend had
halitosis, biting your fingernails, scratching your head, and any of
numerous other nervous habits.

10. DON'T retell the book you have just read. You may spoil it
for your listener, and you will certainly bore him if it is a book of
any length. Suggest that the other person read the book, or give him
just a sentence or two of its theme or plot. The author who wrote
the book can tell it better than anyone else. You may enjoy discussing
the author, however, or the setting or situation of the story, if you
are both interested in this.

11. DON'T try to be funny. Witty remarks add life to a conversation, but forced humor is boring, and ridicule has no place whatever in friendly conversation. Some people have a talent for making
amusing remarks, and they are always welcome company. Most of us
are on dangerous ground here, however, and may profitably remember what Joseph Addison said—"good nature is more agreeable in conversation than wit, and gives a certain air to the conversation. . . ."

12. DON'T finish other people's sentences for them, and don't
supply a word for the conversationalist who pauses to think. You
upset your companion's mental balance this way as surely as you
upset his physical balance by pulling the rug out from under his feet.

There is a proverb which says, "Education begins a gentleman;
conversation completes him." With education—knowing—in whatever area, we have content for our conversational needs. Education,
an understanding of good social usage, a controlled voice, and average
personality adjustment are the essentials of satisfying conversational
experience. We may question whether conversational ability truly
"completes" a gentleman (or lady), but we may be sure that it is an
essential part of this completion.

Telephone Conversations

Nearly all we have said in our foregoing discussion of conversation applies, and in part with additional emphasis, to conversation by
telephone. Here the social situation is different, but the factors of
voice, speech, intelligibility, ideas, and suitability-awareness are all
essentially the same.

It would be hard for people today to conceive of life without the telephone. We use it extensively in conducting our social and community lives. In business it is a necessity second only in importance to the businessman himself. Little children learn to speak on the telephone almost as soon as they learn to talk. Unlike reading and writing and figuring, this skill does not have to be learned in school. Partly as a result of this extremely casual approach to our use of the telephone instrument, however, our telephone manners are often exceedingly bad and may go uncorrected throughout life.

As in ordinary conversation, a well-modulated and relatively low-pitched voice carries most effectively over the wire. Careful enunciation and unhurried speech are most important. Your listener has no clue to what you are talking about except your words. Facial movements—the smile, the frown, the bored look—will not carry over the wire. Your tone of voice will express your mood (we may think of it as a verbal handshake) and your words must be understood in order to convey your meaning. Remove the pipe or cigarette from your lips while you are talking. If you are a gum-chewer, don't try to talk through your gum. If you are a pencil-nibbler, save the pencil for after your telephone conversation.

IF YOU ARE MAKING A CALL

Call the correct number. Ogden Nash comments unhappily in one of his poems: [1]

> Some one invented the telephone,
> And interrupted a nation's slumbers,
> Ringing wrong but similar numbers.

Fortunately, perhaps, we all experience the annoyance of receiving wrong-number calls, and such experience should fortify our own efforts to avoid making similar mistakes.

Identify yourself at once in both social and business situations. Be specific and clear as to whom you are calling. The correct opening for a nonbusiness telephone conversation is,

Hello, this is Jane Hall. May I speak with Mrs. Waters, please?

[1] Ogden Nash, "Look What You Did, Christopher!" *Many Long Years Ago* (Boston, Little, Brown & Co., 1945).

Or if Mrs. Hall is an older woman and the relationship is not a very close one, she may say,

Hello, this is Mrs. Hall. May I speak with Mrs. Waters, please?

If Mrs. Waters is quite a bit younger than Mrs. Hall, the opening would be,

Hello, this is Mrs. Hall. May I speak with Harriet (or Harriet Waters), please?

A man opening a social conversation announces himself with "This is Tim Dale." An older man, in calling a very young woman, may prefer to say, "This is Mr. Dale."

Close acquaintances, in social life or in business, will simply say,

Jean, this is Mary Rose.

or

Jim? Bill Patman speaking.

In business, titles are used by women, by men in calling women, and by professional people. A woman says,

This is Mrs. Atwood of the Fairway Furniture Company.

or

This is the Fairway Furniture Company; Mrs. Atwood speaking.

A man, calling a woman, substitutes Mr. for the Mrs. in the above examples. Calling another man, he simply says "Atwood," dropping the title.

A medical doctor will usually, in business or social life, announce himself by saying, "This is Dr. Jones." Socially, however, he may prefer to say, "This is Tom Jones."

Conclude your call with a simple "good-bye." Ordinarily, the person who initiates the call is the one to conclude it. Close acquaintances readily fall into current jargon endings—"Bye for now," "Take care," "Be seeing you," "So long, now," and even the infantile "Bye-bye." There is nothing wrong with these except that they are habit-forming, and you may use them thoughtlessly in a social situation demanding formality.

IF YOU ARE ANSWERING THE CALL

"Hello" is the accepted answer to the nonbusiness home call. Occasionally you may hear the answering voice say "Yes?" or "Mary Jones here" or "Are you there?" or even "Talk!" These are Canadian-English-Continental imports and translations. They may startle you, but in their own environment they are quite accepted and routine. Usually, when an individual has been in this country a short time the American "Hello" is adopted and this problem disappears.

When the call is intended for someone else, you say,

> Yes, surely you may speak with him.

or

> Yes, indeed. Just hold the wire a moment.

It is also quite correct but a matter of family preference for the telephone answerer to add the routine request,

> May I ask who is calling, please?

Usually the caller volunteers this information without being asked. It is important for children to learn *not* to pick up the phone and demand "Who's this?"—much too brusque and grating an opening for a friendly conversation.

When the call comes at a busy moment, it is quite proper for you to ask permission to call back later. You may be serving dinner, or entertaining guests, or bathing the baby, or in the midst of any of the innumerable small crises of daily living, and your friend will understand. It is imperative, however, that you do not fail to call back. Failure to do so could be interpreted as an intentional insult.

If the asked-for person is not available, the person who answers the telephone should say,

May I take a message for him, please?

or

Would you like me to have her call you when she comes in?

In either case, a note pad with pen or pencil should be close to the telephone for the careful jotting down of messages or telephone numbers.

The proper way to answer a business call is to give the firm name first, and then, if other than the switchboard operator, the person answering gives his or her own name. The sequence would be somewhat as follows:

SWITCHBOARD OPERATOR: Good morning. Berger's Department Store.
CUSTOMER: Good morning. I would like to talk to someone in the china department, please
SWITCHBOARD OPERATOR: Thank you. I will connect you.
CHINA DEPARTMENT: China department. Miss Parker speaking. May I help you?

In answering an office call, the secretary answers her employer's telephone with,

Dean Atkins office. Miss Jones speaking.

If the employer is in conference and cannot be disturbed, Miss Jones then says,

I'm sorry, Dean Atkins is not available right now. May I help you?

or

May I take a message?

She always explains that the Dean is not available *before* saying, "Who is calling, please?" or "What did you want to speak to him about?" This avoids giving the appearance that the secretary has instructions to rebuff this individual. She should, of course, always obtain all important information to pass on to her employer when he is again free to talk.

If an employer is out of town, or out of the office, the secretary explains this to each person who calls and offers to take a message. She is careful not to give out details of his business or plans. He may prefer to keep these out of the hands of his competitors.

When information requested in a business call is not immediately available, it is courteous to explain to the waiting listener that it will take a few minutes to locate the information. He may be asked if he prefers to remain on the wire or to have the information telephoned back to him. This avoids the long, long silence in which the person at the far end of the line does not know if he has been cut off, forgotten, or shoved aside.

Business people who place calls through their secretaries or other office personnel must be instantly available to take over the call when the contact has been reached. To require a listener to wait under these circumstances is inconsiderate and unmannerly and by some is regarded as insulting.

DOS AND DON'TS OF TELEPHONE ETIQUETTE

1. DO keep a note pad and pen or pencil near the telephone so the person calling won't have to wait while you find one.

2. DO make sure you have (and use) the right number so you will not disturb strangers.

3. DO try to call people at times convenient for them—not at their dinner hour, not late in the evening if you know them to be early retirers, not early in the morning if you know them for late risers. Be considerate.

4. DO make your conversations brief if you know you are talking to a usually-busy person.

5. DO ask whether the other person is free to talk if you expect a long conversation. Offer to call back at some other time if there is any question about this.

6. DO be specific when leaving a message. Be sure the person receiving your call understands your name. If it is a business call, give your reason for calling and specify a time and place, with telephone number, where you can be reached.

7. DO space your calls on a party line so others on the line may have a chance to use the telephone.

8. DO put the receiver down gently when your call is finished. A banged-down receiver gives a "good riddance" impression if your contact at the other end of the wire happens to hear it.

9. DO pay for toll calls when you are at the home of a friend or relative. If you are calling your own home, you can usually arrange to reverse the charges and thus avoid this sometimes embarrassing problem. If this is not possible, ask the operator what the toll was and leave the coin unostentatiously near the phone—perhaps on the note pad, on which you might write "Thank-you" and sign your name.

10. DON'T make a guessing game of your call. Announce who you are immediately and to whom you wish to speak.

11. DON'T say, "Who is this?" or "What number is this?" if you suspect you have the wrong party. Instead, say, "Is this Adams 4-6000?" or "Is this the Perkins residence?" and when you are assured that it is not, say, "Oh, I'm *so* sorry. I have the wrong number. Please excuse the call."

12. DON'T be ill-tempered if you are at the receiving end of a wrong number. If the caller is confused, embarrassed, or brusque and demands, "Is this you, Mamie?" you answer, "No, I'm sorry, there is no Mamie here. You must have the wrong number." Your caller then may apologize and hang up, or he may be flustered and say, "Well, who's this?" Your cue is then to ask, "What number is it you wish?" The caller we are describing may hang up abruptly, or he may tell you the number he is trying to reach. You repeat that he has the wrong number and then you hang up. Don't ever give your name, address, or other information to strangers who call without making their reasons clear. This is a precaution against the misuse of the phone by people whose purposes range from curiosity to criminal intent. Children, especially, should be warned and taught to handle this situation.

13. DON'T shout over the telephone. People tend to do this especially when making long-distance calls. Shouting is not only unnecessary, but actually lessens the intelligibility of the conversation. Use your normal talking voice and if you make any change, slow down a bit.

14. DON'T let small children answer the telephone until they have been taught to do so courteously. Your friends will of course excuse the children, and you, for the childish faults, but nevertheless the result is usually annoyance. Cuteness seldom carries well over a telephone wire.

15. DON'T make business calls, if this can be avoided, *at business closing times*. You may get hurried attention, and you may cause a commuter to miss his train.

16. DON'T use the office telephone for social calls. Some business offices forbid this practice and nearly all frown on it. Social chit-chat in an office annoys others who are working. This is as true of the employer as of his staff, and in his case it sets a bad example.

17. DON'T leave your desk without arranging for someone to take your calls. Leave word where you can be located and when you will return.

18. DON'T keep a visitor waiting while you talk on and on. Explain to your telephone caller that you have a visitor and that you will call back. Then be sure that you do so.

4

In-Public Manners

The title *In-Public Manners* does not imply that we can have one set of manners for home use and another set for use when in public. The manners we practice at home with the family will be the same as those we display away from home, whether we wish it to be this way or not. Party manners, like cheap veneer, peel off at the first hard rub. Only the genuinely poised and confident person can maintain a poised and confident attitude in public situations. Only the person whose home behavior is unfailingly courteous will be unfailingly courteous when in public.

In so far, then, as we are the same person regardless of our surroundings, our home or private manners will also be our public manners. The two worlds are not identical for any of us, however, and our private manners are almost never adequate for meeting public situations. The person who feels self-conscious in public is likely to appear rude and awkward and often draws attention to himself or herself by conspicuous behavior. The loud-talking, gum-chewing individual whose costume is extreme in color and style, who appears to enjoy crude and violent horseplay and public love-making is in reality an insecure person, who behaves this way through ignorance.

Deliberately conspicuous behavior in public is grossly ill-mannered behavior; it is one of the worst offenses against good taste and will badly damage the offending individual's status in his or her

44

community. Obviously, a chapter on acceptable public manners will not be likely to influence a deliberately conspicuous person. It can, however, help the person who does not wish to be conspicuous through ignorance. For this reason, the present chapter will discuss the "small niceties" and larger courtesies that add up to pleasant and mannerly public behavior.

Since the *public* world is such a very big place, we will divide public situations for our own convenience into those which occur as we are *in transit*—moving from where we are to where we want to be; those which occur as we are *eating in public*—in restaurants; and those which occur where people are *assembled to be entertained or enlightened*—in the theater, movie house, concert hall, and so on.

IN TRANSIT

Europeans have frequently remarked that the people of the United States never stop moving about; they say that we are always going somewhere. We are insatiable travelers and globe-trotters whenever world conditions permit us to travel freely (travel etiquette is separately discussed in the chapter on that subject). We are also given to daily patterns of restless movement within commuting and shopping range of our homes. All of our contacts on these local travels are public contacts, even if we use our private cars, and specific questions of behavior may arise.

ON THE STREET

Should a man always walk on the outside (the curb side) of the pavement, or should he walk so that the woman is always on his right?

In Europe, a man walking with a woman customarily keeps the woman to his right, regardless of curb location. In this country, however, tradition has long maintained that the man should keep to the outside, or curb side, of the pavement. In order to remain in this position he moves behind his companion as necessity requires when they change the direction of their walk. The woman automatically moves to the right or the left in response to his change of position. If one man is walking with two women, he continues to take the outside position; he does not walk between them. One woman walking with two men, on the other hand, does take the middle position.

Who is expected to speak first when acquaintances meet in passing?

It is the woman's role to speak first if there is any hesitation about recognition. Usually both people are likely to speak almost in unison, and this is one of numerous situations in which friendliness is of more importance than the strict adherence to rule. Say, "Hello, Jane," or "How do you do, Mr. Jones?" or "Good morning."

When does a man offer his arm to a woman?

If a man and a woman are walking together in a crowd, the man offers his arm to the woman to prevent their being separated. A man will also offer his arm to an older woman when she is crossing the street, climbing steps, and so on. The man does *not* grip the woman's arm and push her along ahead of him. He crooks his elbow and allows his companion to slip her hand comfortably through. Women, unless they are infirm, should not hang heavily on a man's arm.

It sometimes happens that a man or woman finds it necessary to assist a blind person on the street. In this situation it is very important to remember that the handicapped person needs to be led, or guided, and does not wish to be pushed. The blind person prefers to have you place his or her hand through your arm, or on your shoulder, and he can then walk with you safely and comfortably. You should of course mention steps or other obstacles as you come to them, and you should do this as casually and unobtrusively as possible.

When does a man tip, or remove, his hat?

Since many men now often go hatless, this problem does not arise as frequently as in the past. However, for the man who wears a hat, custom has not changed.

A man tips his hat . . .

. . . when he greets a woman he knows as they pass each other on the street or in other public places.

. . . when he is walking with a woman and the woman greets a friend (man or woman) who is passing by.

. . . when he is walking with another man who greets a woman as she is passing by. If the friend being greeted is a man instead of a woman, none of the men tip their hats.

. . . to a clergyman, although he does not ordinarily tip his hat to other men.

. . . in a public situation, whenever he has occasion to say "please," "thank you," or "excuse me." For example, if he finds it necessary to ask directions from a stranger, he tips his hat as he says, "please tell me if I am near West Street." If he is walking on a crowded street and bumps into, or is shoved into, another person, man or woman, he tips his hat as he says "excuse me." If the person entering a building ahead of him holds the door for him, he tips his hat as he says "thank you."

A man removes his hat . . .

. . . when he stops to talk with a woman he knows on the street or in other public places.

. . . when he is walking with a woman and the woman stops to talk with another woman. If his companion stops to talk with another man, he does not remove his hat.

. . . when women are present in any close-quarters situation where removing his hat is practicable—club, hotel, apartment house elevators, foyers. He usually *does not remove his hat* in public buildings such as railroad or bus terminals, in office building corridors and elevators, nor does he remove his hat when walking through hotel lobbies and department stores, or in other stores.

Hat-wearing customs are sometimes dictated by strong cultural and religious convention. It is always wise to remember this before assuming that the nonconformist in your orbit is necessarily the unmannerly boor you are inclined to think him. He may be courageously conducting himself according to the prescribed terms of his belief.[1]

[1] For instance, Jewish religious ritual requires the "covered head" for men in many situations where non-Jewish custom regards hat-wearing as unmannerly. Thus, in parts of our country where the orthodox Jewish population is numerous it is not at all unusual to find men wearing hats or skull-caps to meals and wearing them, also, whenever they are in their own or others' homes.

Withhold judgment, therefore, until you know what you are judging.

Who passes first through the doorway of buildings?

In general, when a man and woman are entering a building together, the man opens the door and then stands aside to allow the woman to enter first. However, convenience, safety, and strength must be considered, especially in public buildings where the doors are frequently heavy and hard to hold open. In this situation it is better for the man to go through first, forcing the door open and holding it thus while the woman follows him. If the door is a *revolving door*, the woman enters first and the man puts the door in motion for her. If the door is an *elevator door*, the woman enters first and the man follows and gives the floor number to the operator. When the desired floor has been reached, the man stands aside and allows the woman to leave the elevator ahead of him.

IN A PUBLIC CONVEYANCE

Who enters bus, subway, streetcar, train first? Who leaves first?

The man *steps aside to allow the woman he is with to enter* a public conveyance first. He *does not step aside* to allow other women to enter, although it is thoughtful of him to be alert to elderly or infirm women or men who may be at a disadvantage in the crowd. In *leaving* the vehicle, the man gets off first so that he is in a position to assist the woman when she alights.

When does a man give up his seat in a public conveyance to a woman?

A man retains his seat in a crowded vehicle unless the woman who enters and stands near him is . . .

. . . elderly.

. . . carrying a baby or attempting to control a small child, or is burdened with packages, or is too short to reach the hand-straps easily.

. . . physically disabled (this would of course be true for any disabled person, man or woman).

In other words, the man gives up his seat to anyone who obviously needs it more than he does, and this same courtesy applies to young women as well. In accepting the seat, the person receiving the courtesy shows appreciation by saying "thank you." If this is a woman and she is accompanied by a man, her escort also says "thank you" and tips his hat as a gesture of gratitude and appreciation.

IN A PRIVATE CAR

Who enters and leaves an automobile first?

The man customarily opens the car door and allows the woman to precede him into the vehicle. If the situation involves one man who is driving and one woman, the man opens the front door on the passenger side and seats his companion, then goes around the car to the driver's side to take his own seat. If the woman is going to drive, the man first seats her in the driving seat and then goes around the car to take his own seat beside her on the passenger side.

In leaving the car, the man steps out first, then goes around the car to the woman's side, opens her door and stands aside while she leaves the vehicle or assists her in leaving it.

Should traffic conditions be hazardous, however, the man should first excuse himself to his companion and then enter the car ahead of the woman if necessary to avoid exposing himself to the danger of the open street. In leaving the car under these circumstances, the man leans across the woman to open the door on her side. The woman steps out of the car and the man follows her.

What do we mean when we speak of driver courtesy?

Courteous people are nearly always law-abiding people. Traffic rules may be thought of as a behavior code "with teeth." The teeth —or penalties—are necessary because driving is a life-and-death matter and the discourteous driver kills and maims other people as well as himself. Depending upon our point of reference, it is possible to say that Americans are flagrant law-breakers—how often do they abide by the posted speed limits within towns and cities? Or we may say that they are almost universally law-abiding and cooperative— how often do we see them intentionally driving through a red light? This is a confused conduct pattern and it is probably directly related to the degree of danger recognized by the driver.

Driving, in our time, has emotional and character significance as well as very practical value. In this respect, it is perhaps a little like the drinking of alcoholic beverages. Our reasons for what we do in either situation have very deep roots, and our driving and drinking habits and manners provide a significant key to what we are. Anxious parents might well take a look at the driving behavior of their sons' and daughters' friends if they wish to know what kind of people these are. The name-calling, road-hogging, speeding, weaving, cop-avoiding, tail-riding driver may prove an angry, impatient, intolerant, thoughtless, and unkind son or daughter-in-law—a devious, unpredictable, and unstable personality.

It is always possible, of course, that discourtesies arise from ignorance. For that reason we are listing here a few dos and don'ts of driver courtesy:

1. DO, in a tight situation, yield the right of way regardless of who is legally entitled to this right. In other words, practice the rule of courtesy as in nondriving situations—*be considerate!* You cannot know *why* the other driver is behaving peculiarly. Perhaps he is ill. Perhaps he is lost. Perhaps his car is out of control. Perhaps he is drunk. In any case, *your personal honor* (or ego) *is not involved.* If you cannot avoid becoming emotional about how the other fellow drives, *you should not be driving a car.*

2. DON'T be a highway show-off. This is a form of boasting and is in extremely bad taste. It is a sign of immaturity and would be ludicrous if it were not so gruesomely dangerous. You may be a skillful driver—so are millions of other people. United States streets and highways are no place for amateurs. But if you feel that you need to *prove* your skill, you are an amateur and *you should not be driving a car.*

3. DON'T be a one-arm driver. The young man who drives with one arm on the steering wheel and one arm around his companion (and the young woman who not only permits this behavior but encourages it by sitting so close to the driver that he would be

powerless to avert tragedy in an emergency) is indulging in a form of public exhibitionism. His conduct in other areas of life is suspect and *he should not be driving a car*.

4. DON'T be a tail-rider. Don't follow the car ahead so closely that you can't avoid spying on its occupants. You would not think of staring in the windows of your neighbor's home—or *would* you? Close following of this sort leaves you wide-open to such a question and to its implications. To say that close following is also highly dangerous should be unnecessary because it is so obvious. This discourtesy causes a large proportion of all accidents. The confirmed close-follower *should not be driving a car*.

5. DON'T blow your horn except in a real emergency. Skillful drivers and considerate people very very rarely need to use the horn. The person who taps the horn impatiently the instant that a stoplight changes to green is the same person who walks through a train leaving car-doors open behind him. He is the same person who makes biting comments to or about other people at the slightest provocation. This is the practical joker who finds pleasure in the discomfort of other people. He or she is mean, ego-centered, and psychologically a bad risk. This person *should not be driving a car*.

In-public Eating

In-public eating, or eating out, is one of America's most frequent amusements. We eat out to obtain a change from home cooking, to save labor, to experience different or exotic flavors and customs, or just to be near other people. At no time do good or poor manners show so plainly as at the table—whether in a restaurant or at home. How we eat, how we talk, our posture and our appearance at table—all are important in this special social situation.

Basic familiarity with the implements and techniques necessary to mannerly dining is discussed in the three chapters called *At Table*. Appearance will be discussed briefly in the chapter on good business manners. In-public eating introduces a few special situations, however, and these we will cover in the present chapter. Let us assume that two unmarried couples—Joe and Jean, Bruce and Betty—are dining together in a restaurant.

ENTERING THE RESTAURANT

They enter the restaurant. There is a coat-checkroom near the door. The men ask the women if they wish to leave their coats or wear them to the table. Betty wishes to check her coat. Bruce helps her to remove it and checks it for her. Joe and Bruce then check their own coats and hats. Jean prefers to wear her coat to the table, where Joe will help her slip it off and drape it over the back of her chair. If there were no checkroom, Joe and Bruce would hang their coats wherever space was provided, or, if necessary, they would lay them over a vacant chair, and both women would wear their coats to the table.

The two couples wait at the entrance to the eating area for the headwaiter or hostess to seat them. When this functionary signals them to follow, Jean and Betty go first, and Joe and Bruce follow them. If there were a considerable age difference between the women, the younger woman would step aside to allow the older woman to precede her. A younger man would do the same if he were in the company of a much older man.

If there is no headwaiter or hostess, one of the men—the host, of course, if there is one—leads the way into the dining area and selects a table.

SEATING AT A RESTAURANT TABLE

The headwaiter draws out a chair which he presumably considers the choice seat at the table. Since Jean is first in line, she goes to this chair and the headwaiter seats her. If there is a hostess instead of a headwaiter, the hostess merely indicates the chair and Joe will complete the seating. In this situation Betty will be seated by Bruce in the chair opposite Jean's; Joe will sit in the chair at Jean's left (thus keeping his date to his own right); and Bruce will sit in the chair at Betty's left. The diagrams on page 55 illustrate suitable seating arrangements for small groups in restaurant situations.

If there is neither headwaiter nor hostess, Joe and Bruce select the chairs for Jean and Betty which the men consider desirable. These would preferably be out of the line of traffic in so far as this is possible. If a view, either interior or exterior, is involved, they would seat the women to enjoy this view.

If a woman is entertaining another woman, she directs her guest to the most desirable seat. If the party is a numerous one, the party hostess (or host, if there is no hostess) leads the way to the table and directs the seating; or the seating may be taken care of by place cards which are arranged before the guests are brought to the table. In a group situation, each man seats the woman to his right. He does this immediately after the headwaiter or host begins to seat the "first lady." If the number of guests is uneven, the man seats the woman to his right first, and then the one on his left if she has not already completed the act of seating herself. If a husband and wife are entertaining a lone woman guest, the husband seats the guest first and then assists his wife.

The following suggestions can help to simplify this frequently-fumbled restaurant-seating problem:

1. Someone must take charge. In a party situation, this will be the party-hostess, if there is one; otherwise, the host. In a nonparty large-group situation, one couple assumes the lead and suggests a seating arrangement, observing the reminders listed below.

2. The place of honor is at the right. A woman guest of honor is seated to the right of the host. A man guest of honor is seated to the right of the hostess.

3. Unmarried couples are seated by having the woman to the right of her escort whenever this is possible. (See *Diagram A-3*, page 55.)

4. Married couples are seated opposite each other or are separated and seated next to other couples. They are not seated next to each other if this can be avoided. (See *Diagrams A-2* and *C-2*, page 55.)

5. Place cards are very useful if a party of eight or more is involved. These should be handled in the same way as place cards used for a dinner party served in the home. (See page 91.)

6. Seating oneself at table from the left side of the chair can eliminate much confusion.

Jean and Joe, Betty and Bruce are now seated at table as in *Diagram A-3*. Jean and Betty lay their *gloves and bags* on their laps, or beside them on the sofa or bench if they are sitting in an alcove. They *do not* lay them on the *table*, and preferably they do not put them on the floor. In some situations, however, if the bags are very large or bulky, or if the seating arrangements are cramped, the floor may offer the only space available for accessories, and then of course it must be used.

The waiter or waitress gives each of them a menu, fills their water glasses, and may ask them if they wish cocktails. When young people ask for alcoholic drinks at a restaurant, they must be prepared to show proof of their age to the waiter. The legal drinking age varies in different states, and it is a very serious infringement of the law for the restaurant to serve drinks to underage patrons. The penalties for such an infringement are quite severe, and a waiter or waitress should never be asked to make an exception. Adding cocktails or wine to a restaurant meal greatly increases the cost of the meal, and guests should always wait for their host or hostess to suggest drinks before bringing up the subject. Sometimes the table waiter handles the drink orders as well as the meal orders, and sometimes the wine steward is summoned to take the drink orders. In the latter case, the wine steward usually receives a separate tip.

GIVING THE ORDER

If the waiter does not pass out the menus, Bruce or Joe does so. Jean and Betty wait to have a menu handed to them before examining it. Then all four discuss the order. Bruce and Joe take the lead in making suggestions (sometimes aided by the waiter), and from their suggestions Jean and Betty get an idea of the price dinner their escorts are considering. Traditionally, the women tell the men what they would like to eat, and the men give the order to the waiter. However, the waiter frequently consults the women directly about the details of their order and they answer him directly.

The menu may list only *à la carte* service—requiring dish-by-dish selection, with a separate price indicated for each article of food. It may list only *table d'hôte* service—requiring complete-meal selection, with price indicated for the meal as a unit and remaining the same regardless of whether or not all the courses are ordered and consumed. Blue plates, club meals, shopper's and businessmen's lunches, are forms of table d'hôte service. The menu may also list both types of service and the patrons make their choice between these.

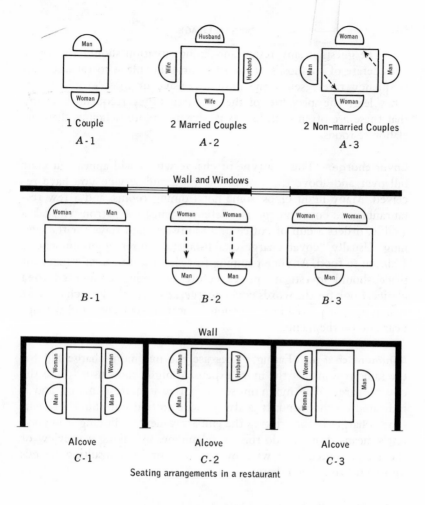

1 Couple
A-1

2 Married Couples
A-2

2 Non-married Couples
A-3

Wall and Windows

B-1

B-2

B-3

Wall

Alcove
C-1

Alcove
C-2

Alcove
C-3

Seating arrangements in a restaurant

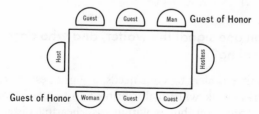

Guest of Honor

Guest of Honor

Seating arrangements for entertaining at home or in public

SEATING ARRANGEMENTS FOR ENTERTAINING
AT HOME OR IN A RESTAURANT

55

The guests in any restaurant-dining situation should always be considerate of the host's or escort's purse. People who eat out with frequency rarely select the most expensive or most exotic dishes. They learn the specialties of the restaurants they frequent, knowing that these are often both less expensive and more delicious than the elaborate foods.

Cover charge. This is a type of charge which will appear on your bill over and above the cost of the food and service you have received. Many night clubs, some hotel dining rooms, and a few restaurants use a cover charge as a defense against the patron who takes a table, orders a cup of coffee or a sandwich, and stays for the evening. Usually "cover charge establishments" offer entertainment in addition to food. Anyone planning to visit a food-plus-entertainment place should investigate prices before becoming committed to a choice. Look for the words *cover charge, cover,* or the French *couvert* which may be posted inconspicuously near the entrance and will appear also on the menu.

Minimum charge. Eating places use the minimum-charge bill for the same reason that the more expensive night clubs usually use the cover charge. The minimum-service price is quite common and is indicated on the menu. It is always wise to find out about a restaurant's charges before risking the embarrassment of finding it beyond one's means. You can do this by telephone, by taking a preview of the menu posted in a window or door, or by consulting friends known to have dined there.

YOUR RESTAURANT MANNERS

How can one signal the waiter, and who does the signaling?

If the waiter is alert to your needs, a slight gesture of the hand and an inquiring look will usually bring him to your table. If he is turned away from you, but is within easy hearing distance (at the next table, perhaps), you may call him by saying, "Waiter!" Call a waitress by the term *Waitress*, not *Miss*. If a man and a woman are together at a table, the man does the signaling. If the woman wishes the waiter's attention, she asks the man to signal. If there is a host-guest situation, the guest—either man or woman—asks the host to handle the situation. Should the waiter be out of sight or beyond easy calling distance, you may ask any other waiter who is near you to please let your waiter know he is needed.

Who should be first to begin eating at a restaurant meal?

The hostess begins, if there is one. If a man and woman are dining together, the woman begins.

What does one do if some part of the place setting is not clean? IF AT A FRIEND'S, "ACCIDENTALLY" DROP IT ON THE FLOOR.

First, *don't* wipe it with your napkin! Ask the waiter to replace it for you and make your request as inconspicuous as possible.

What does one do if a napkin or piece of silverware is dropped on the floor?

First, *don't pick it up*! Call the waiter's attention to it. He will remove it and replace it. If the object should be in the direct line of traffic and a danger to others, you may unobtrusively shove it to one side with your foot until the waiter has taken care of it.

What does one do with cigarette ashes if no ash tray is provided?

First, *don't use your saucer, cup, or plate for an ash tray*! As soon as the lack is noticed, signal the waiter and ask for ash trays. Preferably, check for an ash tray before lighting your cigarette.

When the meal is finished, who suggests that it is time to leave?

In a man-woman date situation, the man will usually make this suggestion, since he knows the plans for the evening. If the couple are both aware of the plans, however, or if there are no further plans, the woman may suggest that they leave. In a host or hostess situation this is the prerogative of the person who is entertaining.

TIP
SWANK ENTERTAINMENT — NOT LATE — WHO PROCEEDES FIRST

How much may a woman touch up her face at the table?

If there will be no time or opportunity to use the dressing room before leaving the restaurant, a woman may inconspicuously and briefly apply lipstick while still at the table. It is not good form to apply powder, or to comb the hair, however.

Who helps the woman with her coat when she is ready to leave?

If the coat is draped over the back of her chair, the waiter may pull out the chair and help the woman with her coat. If the waiter does not perform this service, the escort does so. If the woman has checked her coat, her escort reclaims it for her and helps her to put it on before getting his own coat.

Who goes first as a couple leaves the dining area?

The man steps back and allows the woman to precede him from the room.

What does one do when recognizing friends at another table in a restaurant?

Nod and smile when you catch the eye of someone you know. Don't call out or wave violently to get their attention. When leaving (or entering) the restaurant you may stop at a friend's table *very briefly.* If men are seated at the table and a woman stops to speak to someone at the table, the men rise while the visitor is standing there. If the visitor is a man and the men at the table are introduced to him, they rise, shake hands, and resume their seats. If the visitor is already known to them, they do not rise but acknowledge his presence with a smile and a greeting.

How much does one tip the waiter or waitress?

The person who is paying the bill leaves the tip at his place if the bill is to be paid to a cashier. If the bill is presented by the waiter on a small tray, the person who is paying the bill lays his money on the tray and waits for the waiter to return his change. He then leaves the tip on the tray. (See *Tipping*, page 227.)

The Entertainment Hall

A third, common form of in-public social situation exists in theater-movie-concert-lecture experiences. Some behavior dilemmas are peculiar to these situations.

1. Arrive on time! This is especially important for theater-concert-lecture situations. If you are late, do not expect the ushers to allow you to take your seat until a scene or performance break occurs. Continuous movie performances make timing less important here. However, it is thoughtful to wait for some less-exciting sequence before forcing a whole row of people to rise and allow you to pass. The brief moment during which you obstruct their view may be the key moment of the picture.

2. Avoid talking, audible gum-chewing, program-rattling, or nervous moving about. This is especially important in performances where each word or musical note is of great significance. Unnecessary noise is also extremely irritating during the showing of a movie and can spoil the picture for nearby onlookers.

3. Do not rise or put on your coat to depart before the entertainment is over. This is distracting to your seat neighbors who may wish to experience the entertainment to the end.

4. Applaud when applause is indicated but do not break into the middle of a performance with applause. Don't be boisterous about applause and don't be apathetic. Applause is your opportunity to say "thank you," "well-done," or perhaps "very well-done."

5. If it is necessary to pass people already seated in your row, say, "excuse me"; if you happen to stumble or brush against them, the phrases "I am sorry," or "I beg your pardon," are appropriate. Face the stage as you pass in front of people. Those who are seated should stand up to allow you to pass.

6. Women attending theatrical or movie performances are expected to remove their hats after being seated unless the hats are very small and head-hugging. If a woman seated in front of you fails to remove her hat and it obstructs your view, you may quietly and politely ask her to remove it. At concerts and lectures women usually do not remove their hats.

7. If you leave your seat during intermissions, be very sure to return before the entertainment recommences. A person may excuse himself and leave his companion alone briefly during an intermission, taking care to return promptly.

When couples attend an entertainment together they proceed according to a formula not unlike that outlined for restaurant procedure:

Upon entering the entertainment hall, the man presents his tickets at the door and receives stubs as his receipt and seat-reservation guide.

If there is a coat-checkroom in the lobby, the man checks his coat and hat. The woman's coat may be checked, but she more often wishes to wear it to her seat, where the man helps her to remove it and throws it over the seat-back for her.

The man presents his ticket-stubs to the usher, and they go down the aisle with the woman following the usher and the man following the woman. If no usher is available, the man goes down the aisle first, finds the seats, and steps aside for his partner to enter the row ahead of him.

The man occupies the seat closest to the aisle. When a group of two or more couples attend an entertainment together, each man follows the woman he is accompanying into the row, to avoid confusion.

When you are attending the theater, a concert, or a lecture, it is discourteous to leave before the end of the performance. If you find that you must leave, try to time your departure to coincide with some natural break. This is less important when attending a movie, although even here consideration for others should restrain you from rising and blocking the view of the screen at some particularly interesting point in the show.

When the entertainment is ended, the man, being nearest the aisle, steps out first. Then he waits so that the woman may precede him, or walk with him, as they leave. If the crowd is very dense, he may walk ahead to make room for her.

The Smoker's Good Manners

The smoking of tobacco has health implications as well as manners significance in today's social situations. The health aspect is beyond the scope of this book, but the smoker should not forget that his or her activity may be affecting the well-being of others. Smoking, when it takes place in public, is, like the driving of a car, not a right but a privilege. It may be enjoyed just so long as it does not interfere with the rights and privileges of others. It is probably true that most people do not object to moderate amounts of tobacco smoke in the air they breathe. However, if they do object, the polite and considerate smoker will immediately discontinue smoking. Some people are allergic to tobacco smoke. Some people are made physically ill by it. And some people just dislike it—usually intensely. There are places where smoking is both illegal and dangerous. All smokers should observe the following suggestions and precautions.

The considerate smoker will . . .

. . . always ask "Do you mind if I smoke?" when in a confined space such as a private car or a small office.

. . . light a woman's cigarette before his own.

. . . ask for ash trays rather than use the dinnerware.

. . . avoid spilling ashes on floor, table, or dinner cloth.

. . . not throw lighted cigarettes in an unused fireplace.

. . . never put a burning cigarette on a table, mantel, or other piece of furniture, even for a minute. Burned linen and furniture cannot be repaired. This is an expensive mistake.

. . . make certain his cigarette is really out.

. . . not blow smoke, even accidentally, in another person's face. He will make certain that the smoke from the cigarette he has laid down is not making its way into someone's face.

. . . not talk with a cigarette, cigar, or pipe in his mouth—nor will he play bridge with it in his mouth.

No one should smoke . . .

. . . at any religious ceremony, at weddings, christenings, funerals, whether they are held at home or in church.

. . . in the sick room. If the patient is smoking and suggests that you smoke, then it may be suitable for you to do so in moderation.

. . . when dancing.

. . . in a crowded elevator.

. . . where there are "No Smoking" signs—in a court of law, the theater (except the lobby), the concert hall, museums, libraries, buses, most department stores (especially fitting rooms), etc.

. . . when entering an office for an interview or to keep an appointment. Do not smoke until invited to do so. Business firms have different policies as regards smoking. Always obey the policy.

Women should not smoke while walking on city streets, and men should not smoke while walking with women on city streets.

SMOKING AT TABLE

If you are a guest at dinner in the home of a friend, you will know whether you are permitted to smoke during the meal by the presence or absence of an ash tray as a part of your place setting. Today very few hostesses fail to provide cigarettes and ash trays for their guests. Do not go to a table with a lighted cigarette and do not start smoking immediately after being seated. If no ash trays are provided on the table, it is better to wait until the end of the meal to smoke.

The cigar-smoker should smoke only at coffee time, and then only if the hostess indicates that she has no objection to the strong odor. Before smoking he should make sure that he has a large ash tray available.

The pipe-smoker, like the cigar-smoker, should confine his smoking to the meal's end. Pipes may be smoked even after a formal dinner—provided the hostess has expressed no objections.

5

Funerals

When a funeral must be planned, those who are closely related to the deceased will consult with the family's spiritual advisor and with the funeral director concerning the details.

Either the family or the funeral director issues the death notice to the newspapers with the time and place of the final rites. Any specific requests of the family with regard to flowers should be included. If the family desires a private ceremony, time and place of the funeral should be omitted from the death notice. When these are included, however, all who knew the deceased socially or professionally should make an effort to be present.

When a private funeral has been indicated, relatives and close friends are notified of details by telephone. Other friends should go to the home, leave a card, and offer to assist in any way. Avoid going into details when expressing sympathy. A few sincere words will be welcome and adequate.

If the funeral notice reads "please omit flowers," friends should abide by the family's wishes. In lieu of flowers a donation may be sent to a specified charity. In this case, the check is sent to the indicated charity with a note saying that this is in memory of the deceased. The charity will notify the family of your gift.

If flowers are sent, they should be addressed "To the funeral of ——." The card accompanying the flowers should have the full name of the sender. It should not read, for example, just "Jane and Tim." The words "With deep sympathy" may be used, although the name alone is all that is necessary.

When flowers are permitted, the family of the deceased should designate someone to list the floral pieces and describe each on the back of the card accompanying it. The director at the funeral home may have this done. This information is necessary to the family later when writing their notes of thanks. Cards should always be removed before the flowers are displayed.

All expressions of sympathy should be acknowledged by handwritten notes on white notepaper and should be sent by the closest relative. Only a few lines are necessary, such as, "Thank you for your kind note of sympathy and the beautiful basket of pink carnations." Engraved or printed acknowledgments should never be used except in the case of the death of a very prominent person which results in hundreds of messages and flowers to be acknowledged. Even in this situation, handwritten notes would be sent to close friends and relatives.

The fee for the clergyman who officiates is sent to him after the funeral and is accompanied with a letter of appreciation for his assistance and comfort. There is, of course, no fixed amount. This depends upon the financial position of the family. After a church funeral a check is sent to the sexton and the organist.

When attending a funeral, women should wear conservative clothes, avoiding gay hats. Men should wear dark business suits.

Motorists should always give funeral processions right-of-way in order to avoid causing the cars to be separated. For the same reason they should take care not to absent-mindedly "join" the procession.

What social activities may be attended by the family of the deceased is up to the individuals concerned. Probably they will not wish to attend a gay formal party or reception within a period of six months after the funeral. However, a quiet evening with friends or attendance at the theater seldom draws criticism.

6

At Table: Manners and Methods

A young man of good appearance, pleasant voice, and excellent academic rating is being
considered for a public-contact
position in an expanding business
firm. It is lunchtime and the interviewer suggests that they con-
tinue their conversation while having lunch. At the table the young
man is both nervous and hungry. He spears an olive from the relish
tray with his fork while waiting for his order. He gnaws a large stalk
of celery noisily while his companion is talking to him. When the
order arrives, he grips his knife in one hand and his fork in the other
and does not put them down until his plate is empty. As he answers
the interviewer's questions, he gesticulates forcefully with his implements, and when he finally releases them, it is to leave them carelessly on the tablecloth.

The interviewer eats his own lunch hastily and dismisses the
young man as soon as he can. Needless to say, the young man does
not get the job. His keen mind, good appearance, and nice personality cannot outweigh his poor table manners. This is because in our
present-day American culture, table manners are regarded as an
index of social adjustment. We feel that the person who is unmannerly at table will be unmannerly in his other social relationships.
Bad manners suggest lack of consideration for other people and lack

65

of the sense of fitness. Bad manners are ugly manners and ugly manners at table can ruin the appetite and spoil digestion for the companions of the uncouth one.

The young man's table faults and his use of awkward, conspicuous gestures occurred, as most faults in table etiquette occur, because of ignorance. "God may forgive sins," writes Emerson, "but awkwardness has no forgiveness in heaven or earth." This is because awkwardness is unnecessary. It is not difficult to acquire the physical skills needed for easy self-confidence in the social situation of eating. It is not difficult to make these skills habitual. Poise comes through practice. With poise assured, we can concentrate on the human relationships involved. We need not be nervous at lunchtime job interviews, and we can obtain the maximum satisfaction out of both food and company.

Let us start with some basic maxims. Most of these you will have learned in your early childhood—but do you always remember now? An occasional checkup is good for the body, for the spirit, *and* for your social relationships.

DOS and DON'TS at Table

1. DO sit up fairly straight. A sprawling position makes you appear careless, indifferent, and lazy.

2. DO keep your elbows in, not flapping wing-fashion as you cut and eat.

3. DON'T put your elbows on the table while the meal is in progress. During between-course and end-of-meal conversation *one* elbow may be tolerable if it does not shut out the person sitting beside you. Elbows on the table frequently disarrange your own or your neighbor's place setting.

4. DO spread your napkin on your lap when you are seated. If there is a hostess, wait until she has made this move before you follow suit. Large dinner napkins should be left half-folded on the lap. Small napkins may be opened out full-size. Touch the lips with napkin. Usually it is well to do this before drinking, in order to avoid unsightly marks on the glasses or cups. It is assumed that women will quietly have removed lipstick before using the table napkin. At the end of the meal, or if it is necessary to leave the table before the

meal is over, leave your napkin neatly semi-folded (not violently crushed and not crease-folded) at the left side of your place setting. Never fold your napkin after a meal unless you are in a family situation where you know this is expected. Never wad up a paper napkin when you are through with it. Treat it like a cloth napkin and keep it as neat as possible.

    5. DON'T wipe off your own silverware before eating. This would be inexcusable at a friend's home and is insulting to any reputable proprietor. If necessary, call the waiter and ask for clean silver.

    6. DON'T be a silverware or salt-and-pepper twirler. This detracts from your poise, makes you look nervous, and is irritating to the onlooker. It also spreads gritty salt and pepper over the table and sometimes over the floor.

    7. DON'T be tempted to reorganize by pushing the dinner plate and silver away from you; and DON'T draw pictures on the linen with your silverware. This is a knife-thrust right into the heart of your helpless hostess.

    8. DO take a little of every course that is offered and at least make a pretense of eating. *It is impolite to refuse a dish utterly.* Try to develop a taste for all foods. The true cosmopolite likes and is interested in nearly all kinds of foods. The "picky" eater is a poor guest and a disappointment to host and hostess.

    9. DO express some preference for a food when you are asked.

    10. DO say *"no, thank you,"* if you are refusing anything. You may be a bit more miserly with your "yes, thank you's," since it is assumed that you will accept what is offered. You need not say "thank you" for each dish offered by a waiter.

    11. DON'T reach in front of a person to obtain a desired dish. Ask to have it passed.

    12. DON'T use your own silver to remove food from a platter or serving dish. Each dish should have its own spoon or fork. If it does not, ask the hostess or a waiter for assistance.

    13. DON'T help yourself from a dish *first* when you have been asked to pass it—unless the hostess directs you to do so, or unless a confused situation makes this particularly sensible. In this case, ask permission to help yourself before passing it.

    14. DON'T ask the waiter or maid directly for assistance. This is the hostess' prerogative. Speak to the hostess first if you need something and she will speak to the serving personnel.

15. DON'T ask for second helpings when you are a guest, but you are free to accept seconds if they are offered.

16. DO wait until all are served before beginning to eat if eight or fewer persons are at the table. If you are a guest and your hostess urges you to start eating before the food gets cold, do so. Otherwise, let the hostess give the cues. At a banquet, you may begin eating when those next to you have been served.

17. DO be responsible for putting into circulation the dishes near you—rolls, relishes, etc. The hostess will probably suggest this to you, anyway.

18. DON'T help yourself first, and DO pass to the right. This keeps traffic going in one direction and avoids the situation in which some helpless diner finds himself with a dish of olives in one hand and a basket of rolls in the other and not an empty square inch for laying anything down.

19. DON'T bow down over the plate as you eat. The fork doesn't weigh much and can be lifted to the mouth. Sit straight as food is brought to your mouth.

20. DO use a pusher to capture the food on your plate ONLY *if you are adept at this.* Few of us are. The English use a knife for this purpose, but in the United States a small piece of bread is more often used. The bread itself may then be eaten with the fork.

21. DON'T hold food that is ready to be eaten *on your fork or spoon.* Having once picked it up, eat it promptly—and completely; no half-sipping of ice cream from a too-full spoon.

22. DO cut only one or two pieces of meat at a time. It looks greedy, and childish, to do otherwise.

23. DON'T blow on liquid to cool it. The results of this can be disastrous.

24. DON'T dunk in public. In the bosom of your family, let your family decide. This is a very old custom and there is no denying it has some gustatory virtues. However, it can't be made attractive to the onlooker, and it has no place in public or party dining.

25. DON'T leave your spoon in the coffee cup, or the tea cup, or the bouillon cup. You may put out your eye if you drink from a cup with a spoon in it, or worse, you may spill the staining liquid on your hostess's best linen. Place the spoon in the saucer to the right of the cup after you have used it.

26. DON'T stir your beverage too vigorously. This is a nervous mannerism and may slop the liquid over into the saucer, which is the beginning of a series of problems. Coffee, tea, or other beverages may be tested for heat and sweetness by one sip only from the spoon. "Drinking" it by spoonfuls is awkward, noisy, and in poor form.

27. DO eat in small bites, chew quietly with the mouth closed, and wait until the mouth is empty of food before talking. If a question is asked, wait until you swallow your bite before answering.

28. DO slow down if you know yourself as a noisy eater, or if you are customarily way out ahead finishing your meal. The eat-it-on-the-run routine has no place in mannerly dining.

29. DON'T eat your neighbor's salad. Remember that the salad plate and bread-and-butter plate to the left of your dinner plate is always yours.

30. DON'T ever stack your salad plate on top of other plates. In fact, don't stack dishes. This problem belongs to the hostess and her helpers and your efforts to help can only make it worse.

31. DO place used silver on the dish to which it belongs. Never replace silver on the cloth or table once the utensil has been used.

32. DO replace your chair after you get up from the table; or step aside so your escort can do this for you. This helps the flow of traffic in exiting from the dining area.

33. DO contribute to pleasant conversation. Avoid subjects of interest only to yourself. The dinner table is no place to dwell on unpleasant topics of health or disaster. It is no place for anatomical discussions or for tales of food dislikes.

34. DO be well-groomed for the sake of the others who must look at you, and for the sake of your own poise. Dress in keeping with the rest of the group and dress to suit the occasion. If in doubt, ask. Your host, hostess, or a good friend will be glad to help you avoid embarrassment.

35. DO wait for the hostess to make the first move to get up from the table.

Accidents and Emergencies

It was Dickens who discovered, in *David Copperfield*, that "accidents will happen in the best regulated families," and this has been a solace to mankind ever since. There is seemingly no limit to the variety of accidents which can happen at table. They range from a fallen soufflé to violent and even fatal disaster befalling some member of the party. There is probably only one rule that can apply to all persons involved—host and hostess, guests, family members, victim. The rule is "Be calm!" If you are calm, you will remain your usual polite self and you will automatically do the helpful and necessary thing. A few of the more frequent problems with suggested action are listed here:

Coughing, choking, or hiccups. Turn your head, cover your mouth with napkin, handkerchief, or even your bare hand, and make a strong effort to control the paroxysms. If this is impossible, excuse yourself to your hostess and leave the room until you have things under control.

Removing foreign matter from your mouth. This applies to fruit seeds, fish bones, or other inedible material. In the first place, _don't_ attempt to conceal your movements behind a napkin or cupped hand. If eating fruit with a spoon, use the spoon to remove the seeds from your mouth and, preferably, deposit them in the plate alongside your fruit dish. If no plate is provided, you may have to put the seeds back in the fruit dish, but this is unpleasant and a careful hostess will never put you in this situation. If eating fresh fruit, when possible avoid getting stones or seeds in the mouth. When this is not possible, remove the larger stones with your fingers as inconspicuously as possible. Small seeds may be removed from the mouth with a spoon or, if necessary, by hand. Never spit seeds out, at the table. Be as inconspicuous as possible. Fish bones must nearly always be removed with the fingers. This too can be done inconspicuously with a little experience.

Left-handedness. This is neither an accident nor an emergency but it can be a problem for the hostess and for the table companions of the left-handed one. The forewarned hostess will place her left-handed guests at table corners whenever possible. Always set the place for the left-hander in the same way you set places for other guests. He has learned to shift silverware, cups, salad plates, for his own convenience, and usually with a minimum of disturbance. The rule for the hostess and the other guests is "Be nonchalant." This is nature and we can do nothing about it.

Dropped silverware. The social situation will have to be your guide here. If you are in a restaurant, an alert waiter will retrieve the fallen piece and will bring you a fresh one. If the waiter is not alert, signal him, or ask your host to signal him, and your problem will be solved. If you are a guest in a friend's home, your hostess will perform this function for you. Kindness and consideration are to be remembered here. Don't expect your hostess to climb under the table for a spoon you have dropped, and don't leave the object in the traffic lane to be stepped on. Retrieve it yourself and then allow your hostess to procure a clean one for you.

Spilled food or beverage. Small quantities of spilled foods on a table—a few peas, a leaf of lettuce—may be picked up immediately and without comment and returned to the plate where they belong. Larger and messier spill situations will require the attention of the waiter or the hostess. Do not dab your napkin into the spilled material. You will probably just compound the problem. Waiter or hostess will clean up the area with a kitchen cloth and, if necessary, cover it with a clean napkin for the remainder of the meal. Spilled food in a cafeteria may necessitate your calling a waiter to have it cleaned up lest other diners slip on it.

Fly or hair in food. This is almost the ultimate in unappetizing experiences. However, it does sometimes happen. If in a restaurant, try to restrain your distress. Tell the waiter you would like to change your order. He will sense the difficulty and will get the food out of sight as quickly as he can. Do not talk of the experience and spoil the meal for other people. If this happens in a friend's home, eat what you can and plead a poor appetite if the situation is too unpleasant.

WHAT IT IS AND HOW TO EAT IT

The United States is the great cosmopolis of the modern world. Israel Zangwill's dream of America the melting-pot of nationalities was never more true than it is today; and this truth is nowhere more apparent than it is in the nationwide internationalism of our super-markets. The foods of the nations are easily available to most of us at the nearest frozen food department of the nearest shopping center. This is a horizon-stretching experience, and most of us respond to it with enthusiasm. Improved methods of packaging and transportation have further broadened our range of food choice to include fruits, meats, cereals, and vegetables from the farthest parts of our own country—products and dishes once confined to small areas and known as local specialties. These things we may eat now at will—with one proviso. First we must find out what they are and what we are supposed to do with them. Recipes and menus do not come within the scope of a book on social usage. How to handle foods at table, however, is of rapidly increasing importance in the area of table manners. To answer some of these questions, we are including here a thumbnail dictionary on foods and food terms.

THUMBNAIL DICTIONARY [1]

À LA CARTE (ah-lah-cart)—Foods prepared to order; each dish priced separately.

À LA KING—Foods served in a cream sauce, which often contains mush-rooms, green peppers, pimientos.

À LA MODE—This usually refers to pie topped with ice cream. It may also refer to larded, braised beef simmered with vegetables.

À LA NEWBURG—Foods served in a sauce of wine, egg yolk, and cream.

ANCHOVIES—Tiny smoked fish preserved in oil. Usually served on crackers or sautéed bread rounds as a canapé. Can also be used in salads.

ANTIPASTO (ahn-tee-pahs'toe)—Italian name for Italian hors d'oeuvres served as a first course.

APÉRITIF (ah-pay-ree-teef)—Any dry fortified wine. French expression for drink served before meal.

APPLE—A fruit-bowl dessert. Quarter it with your fruit knife and remove the core. Peel and eat with the fingers.

---

[1] The non-English terms used here for which we suggest pronunciation are nearly all French terms. The stress accent on these may safely be placed on the final syllable, thus, *au gratin* (grah-TAN). Where this is not the case, an accent is indicated.

APRICOT—Served fresh, this is another fruit-bowl dessert. Usually too tender to peel, this is a finger food and is eaten away from the pit as neatly as possible.

ARTICHOKE—Served whole, hot or cold, the leaves are pulled off one or two at a time with the fingers; the succulent base portion is dipped in melted butter or mayonnaise and as much of the leaf as is tender is eaten. The inedible leaves are discarded in a neat pile on your plate. When the heart is reached, the spiney tips are cut out with knife or fork and the heart is cut with the fork into bite-size pieces.

ASPARAGUS—French asparagus, its woody ends removed, is sometimes served in long stalks. Eat as much as you can with your fork and leave the remainder.

ASPIC—This is clear jellied meat or poultry broth with or without vegetable seasoning. It is sometimes served as a cold soup or it may be served sliced or molded in a salad.

AU GRATIN (grah-tan)—Sprinkled with cheese, usually browned and crisped.

AU JUS (oh-zhu)—Food served with its natural juices or gravy. Usually applied to meat.

AU LAIT (oh-lay)—Food served with milk.

AU NATUREL (oh-nah-tu-rel)—Food plainly cooked. Undisguised.

AVOCADO—A pear-shaped fruit with a very large pit. Sometimes served cut in half with the stone removed, in which case it is dressed with lime-French dressing and eaten with a spoon. Or it may be peeled, cut up, and served in salads, in which case it is eaten with a fork.

BACON—Use fork. Fingers are permitted when bacon is very dry and crisp.

BABA AU RHUM (bah-bah-oh-rom)—Small cakes with rum flavor and served with whipped cream.

BAKED ALASKA—Ice cream on cake covered with meringue and browned in the oven.

BANANA—Peel all the skin, place on plate, and eat with a fork; or peel partway down and eat the banana bite by bite, using fork (usually eaten this way).

BARBECUE—Roasting whole, usually over direct flame.

BAR-LE-DUC (bahr-le-duk)—Famous jam made of red currants.

béarnaise (bay-ahr-nays)—Rich yellow sauce usually served with meat or fish.

béchamel (bay-shah-mel)—Rich white sauce seasoned with onions, carrots, celery, and sometimes lean ham.

berries—When served whole with the hulls on, the hull of each berry is held in the hand, the berry dipped in sugar or whipped cream and eaten so. Berries served in a fruit dish with cream are, of course, eaten with a spoon.

beurre (ber)—Butter.

beurre noir (ber-nwahr)—Black butter, or very brown butter sauce usually combined with lemon juice and parsley.

beurre roux (ber-roo)—Browned butter.

biscuits—Usually served hot, these should be broken in two and buttered while hot. They should be eaten like bread. (See below.)

biscuit tortoni (biz-kwee tor-toe'-nee)—Rich ice cream packed in small paper cup and sprinkled with chopped almonds or macaroons.

bisque—A rich cream soup, served usually in a cup. (See also *soup*.)

blanc (blahn)—White.

bleu cheese—A mold cheese, like Roquefort, but made from cow's milk.

bombe (bohmb)—Ice cream in bomb shape filled with layers of various ice creams.

bordelaise sauce (bohr-de-lays)—Sauce with seasonings and containing Bordeaux wine.

bouillabaisse (boo-yah-besz)—A thick soup containing five or six varieties of fish cooked together with white sauce.

bouillon (boo-yohn)—A meat broth. When served in a cup it may be drunk, holding one or both handles, or it may be taken from a spoon, dipping the spoon away from you as with soup in a bowl.

braise (brayz)—To brown food, then stew or bake it in steam.

bread—Break bread into small pieces and butter as you eat it. Never place a whole slice of bread on the palm of your hand to butter it. Do not cut bread or rolls with a knife. Don't sit with bread in one hand and fork in the other. Do one or the other at a time.

brioche (bree-osh)—A slightly sweetened rich roll served traditionally with breakfast coffee and eaten with the fingers.

brochette (broh-shet)—A small spit or skewer on which meat is roasted.

If at a picnic, use fingers. At the table, use knife and fork to cut meat away.

BUFFET (boo-fay)—Display of ready-to-eat foods. Self-service from table of assorted foods.

BUTTER—Use a knife to butter bread, toast, and hot breads. Use a fork to put butter on vegetables, except corn, which is buttered with a knife.

CAFÉ (kah-fay)—Coffee.

CAFÉ AU LAIT—Coffee with hot milk.

CAFÉ ROYAL—After-dinner coffee with cognac or other brandy.

CAFFÈ ESPRESSO—Italian dessert coffee. Very black and strong.

CAKE—Slices of large, sticky cake should be eaten with a fork. Dry cake, such as pound cake or fruit cake, is broken up and eaten with the fingers. Tiny cakes and small cookies, such as are served at teas and receptions, are eaten with the fingers.

CAMEMBERT (kah-mahm-bare)—Soft, full-flavored cheese. Usually served with crackers. Spread small portions on cracker to eat.

CANAPÉ (kah-nah-pay) Toasted or fried bread slices of varying size and shape spread with a savory paste or other topping. Served before a meal they are eaten with the fingers. Served at the table they are eaten with a fork. (See also *hors d'oeuvres*.)

CANTALOUPE—When cut in half or in sections, they are eaten out of the shell with a spoon.

CASSEROLE—When an individual casserole is placed on your plate, you may eat directly from it. If there is a cover on it, place the cover on your plate, not on the table. If the casserole is larger and is placed behind your plate, use the large spoon you will receive to serve a small portion at a time onto your plate.

CAVIAR (kav-ee-are)—Seasoned roe, or eggs, of fish. Usually served as a canapé.

CELERY—Should be taken from the relish tray with fingers and placed on the bread-and-butter plate. Break into smaller portions if too long. (See *salt*.)

CHAMPAGNE—Sparkling white wine. A formal dinner wine, usually served on special occasions. Served chilled, from bottle, with neck wrapped in napkin to prevent drip.

CHANTILLY CREAM (shan-tee-yee)—Vanilla whipped cream.

CHARLOTTE (shar-lot)—Cake and pudding-type sweet dessert.

CHARLOTTE RUSSE (roos)—Sponge cake filled with whipped cream or custard.

CHAUTEAUBRIAND (shah-toh-bree-ahn)—Grilled thick steak with brown sauce.

CHEESE—Many kinds of cheese are served as dessert with crackers. Often accompanies fruit. Depending upon type, it may be spread on the crackers, with a knife or fork, or it may be cut or broken into small pieces and eaten with the fingers. If served with pie it is eaten with a fork.

CHEF (shef)—Head cook.

CHERRIES—Fresh cherries are eaten whole. Pits should be removed from the mouth with fingers. Canned cherries are eaten with the spoon and the pits are removed with the spoon and placed on plate.

CHICKEN—Fried or broiled chicken, as well as chicken served in other ways, is eaten with the fork. Fingers may be used at a picnic, in your own home, or when your host or hostess takes the lead in this. Fingers are never used in a hotel dining room. Chicken served "in the basket" is properly eaten with the fingers. Paper napkins are a "must"!

CHUTNEY—A hot, spicy condiment of fruit seasoned with chili, mustard, vinegar. Served with *curries*. (See below.)

CLAM CHOWDER—A thick clam and vegetable soup. Should be served in a soup plate or bowl.

CLAMS—Served as a first course, on the half-shell. Hold shell with the left hand. Lift whole clam from shell with oyster fork, detaching it with the fork. Dip in cocktail sauce which is in container on plate. Eat in one mouthful.

CLUB SANDWICH—These and similar large sandwiches should be cut into smaller portions with your knife before eating. Hold the sandwich down with your fingers as you cut. Eat small sections with the fingers, or if sandwich is "wet," use your fork.

COCKTAILS—This is a loose term applied to premeal drinks and to first-course dishes of shellfish, fruits, or vegetables. The *shellfish cocktails* (shrimp, oyster, etc.) are usually served in small glass bowls, sometimes set in a bed of ice. They are eaten with an oyster fork after dressing them with lemon juice from the lemon wedge and dipping them in the cocktail sauce provided. The *fruit or vegetable cocktails* are eaten from the dish with spoons. "*Juice*" cocktails (tomato or fruit) are usually served in small glasses at the table, and are *sipped*, not gulped. *Alcoholic cocktails* are served before sitting down to the meal. There are numerous varieties, among which Martinis, Daiquiris, Manhattans, are well-known.

Crackers, nuts, or more elaborate hors d'oeuvres are usually served with these cocktails.

COFFEE—May be served at any stage of a "home" meal. Served at a formal dinner, it usually accompanies dessert or follows dessert. Use the spoon sparingly in stirring cream and sugar into your coffee. *Demitasse* is strong black coffee served in small cups after dinner. (See also *café* and *caffè espresso*.)

COMPOTE (kahm-poht)—A dish of stewed fruit.

CONSERVE—Fruit preserve. May be put on the bread and butter plate or on the dinner plate.

CONSOMMÉ (kon-so-may)—A clear soup. (See *bouillon*.)

CORN-ON-THE-COB—If the ear of corn is large, break it. Butter only a small portion at a time, to avoid dripping butter. Hold ends in both hands to eat. Never serve this at a formal dinner.

COUPES (koop)—Ice cream served in a glass with fruit and chantilly cream.

COVER CHARGE—A fixed fee for table service, independent of the charge for food.

CRACKERS, CROUTONS—When served with soup these are placed on the bread and butter plate, or, if small, are dropped directly in the soup, a few at a time.

CREOLE SAUCE—A spicy tomato and green pepper sauce.

CRÊPES (krayp)—French pancakes.

CRÊPES SUZETTE—French pancakes "burned" with brandy and served with a rich sauce.

CROQUETTE (kro-ket)—A molded ground meat or poultry cake rolled in crumbs and deep-fat fried.

CRUMPETS—English breakfast batter cakes.

CURRIES—Highly spiced meat or vegetable dishes usually served with rice and condiments. The condiments—chutney, coconut (shredded), marmalade, chopped pickle, etc.—are served in separate small dishes from which each diner spoons a small portion onto his dinner plate beside the curry and rice. The coconut is sprinkled over the curry.

DÉJEUNER (day-zhu-nay)—French term for lunch or breakfast.

DU JOUR (du-zhur)—Food ready to serve. The specialty for the day.

DEMI (de-mee)—Half.

DEMITASSE (demee-tahss)—Small cup for, or of, after-dinner coffee. Literally translated, the word means half cup. (See also *coffee*.)

EGGS BENEDICT (bay-nay-dick)—Eggs poached and served on toast with ham or tongue and hollandaise sauce.

EGGS FLORENTINE—Eggs poached, served on a bed of spinach and covered with white sauce, then browned in the oven.

ENTRÉE (ahn-tray)—May mean an intermediate course, but usually refers to the main dish.

ESCARGOTS (eskahr-go)—Snails. Eat them from the shell with an oyster fork.

FILET MIGNON (fee-lay meen-yohn)—Tenderloin of beef.

FINGER FOODS—Foods that are properly eaten with the fingers—celery, olives, pickles, radishes, small sandwiches, small cakes, cookies, dry, crisp shoestring potatoes, nearly all forms of bread, and small fresh fruit that is not too juicy.

FISH—Served whole, the backbone is removed as follows. First, remove the head, then, holding fish firm with the fork, slit with the tip of the knife from head to tail. Open and flatten fish, then insert the knife under one end of the backbone and gently lift the backbone out with the fork. Place this on the side of the plate. The fish is then eaten with the fork. Remove any tiny bones that may be left with your thumb and forefinger.

FLAMBÉ (flahm-bay)—A dessert served while in flame from lighted spirits poured over it.

FONDUE (fohn-du)—A cheese dish (like Welsh rabbit). Also meat fondue.

FRAPPÉ (frah-pay)—Frozen, flavored water ice.

FRENCH FRIES—Deep-fat fried potato fingers. Eat with a fork.

FRICASSEE (frik-a-see)—Stewed poultry, veal, or lamb served in a white sauce or gravy.

FROMAGE (froh-mahzh)—Cheese.

GLACÉ (glah-say)—Glazed, iced, frosted.

GRAPEFRUIT—Served cut in half with the sections loosened. Eat with a spoon, preferably a pointed fruit spoon. Do not squeeze out the juice at table.

GRAPES—Eat with the fingers. Hold stem end of grape between the lips. Press with your fingers and the seeds will be left in the skin while the juice and pulp go into your mouth.

GRAVY—Ladle onto meat or potatoes. Do not make a nest with a spoon before helping self to gravy. Put the ladle back in the gravy boat or bowl. *9 (LEAVES POTATOES ON LADLE)*

HAMBURGERS, HEROES, HOAGIES, ETC.—These are all popular sandwiches, often out-size and difficult to eat. Fingers are of course in order for them, but if you can't control them with your hands, try a knife and fork.

HOLLANDAISE (haul-ahn-dayz)—A piquant yellow sauce made with egg yolk, lemon, butter.

HORS D'OEUVRES (or der'vr)—Relishes, appetizers, canapés, tidbits served before a meal with cocktails or as a first course at the table. Use fingers ordinarily.

JELLY, JAM, PRESERVES—Spoon from serving dish and place on bread and butter plate. Use knife to spread on bread or rolls. If it is an accompaniment for meat, such as mint jelly with lamb, put it on your dinner plate and eat it with your fork.

LAIT (lay)—Milk.

LETTUCE—Usually cut and eaten with a fork. If served in wedges, use knife to help in cutting.

LOBSTER—Pull small claws apart with fingers and gently suck from open end. Lift out body meat and cut with knife into bite-size pieces as you eat, dipping each piece into the butter with your cocktail fork. The green or coral matter is also good. Claws should be cracked when served, but you may use nut-cracker to further break them. Then open them with the fingers and lift out the meat with your fork. Ask the waiter for help if you need it.

LYONNAISE (lee-ohn-naiz)—With shredded onions. Usually refers to potatoes served this way.

MACÉDOINE (mah-say-dwan)—A mixture of finely cut-up vegetables. Sometimes used in reference to fruits.

MAÎTRE D'HÔTEL (mai-tr-doh-tel)—Head of the catering department.

MANGO—A soft tropical fruit with a large pit. If served peeled, quartered, and pitted, eat with a fork. If not peeled when served, quarter, hold in place with a fork and pull skin away. Then use fork to cut bite-size pieces as you eat it.

MEAT—Cut one or two pieces at a time. Never cut it all up at once. Avoid a messy plate. (See illustration on page 98 showing how to cut meat.)

MELON—Usually eaten like *canteloupe*. (See above.)

MENU (men'-you)—The bill of fare.

MOUSSE (mooss)—Frozen dessert of whipped cream.

MUSSELS—If served smoked or pickled (as for cocktails), use a toothpick to eat them. If served in the shell, you may use the shell as a spoon by placing the tip of the shell in the mouth and silently sucking out the mussel. Or you may use a cocktail fork to extract the mussel.

NUTS—Use nut spoon to serve yourself from nut dish. Place nuts on bread-and-butter plate or on dessert plate or saucer. Eat with fingers. Never put nuts on the table.

OEUFS (uff)—Eggs.

OLIVES—Eat with your fingers. Bite off, without nibbling, around the stone. Put small stuffed olives in your mouth whole. The olive served in a cocktail is eaten after the glass is drained. Tip the glass until olive (also true for cherry) drops into your mouth. Make several bites of it if it is large.

ONION SOUP—Usually served topped with a round of toast. Grated cheese is passed in a bowl and you sprinkle a spoonful on top of the toast. As with any soup, fill your spoon only three-fourths full and take the soup *silently* from the side of the spoon.

ORANGES—Peel and section neatly or eat like *grapefruit*. (See above.)

OYSTERS—When served raw, on the half-shell, they are eaten like clams on the half-shell. (See *clams*.)

PEACHES—A raw, ripe peach is cut in half and peeled before eating. Eat it with a fork.

PEARS—A raw, ripe pear is quartered, peeled, and seeded, and eaten with the fingers if firm or with the fork if soft and juicy. *APPLE*

PEAS—These are eaten with a fork. You may crush them very slightly to make them easier to handle. *OR HAVE MASHED POTATOES*

PETIT (pe-tee)—Small

PETIT FOURS (foor)—Small cakes.

PICKLES—Place on the butter plate or the side of the dinner plate. Whole pickles or large sections are eaten with the fingers. Mixed pickles are eaten with the fork.

PINEAPPLE—Eaten with spoon if served in a sherbet cup. If served on a flat plate, use a fork. Sometimes served in small wedges to be dipped in powdered sugar, in which case it is eaten with the fingers.

PIZZA (peet-za)—Italian tomato pie. Use a fork for the large pies. Small pies or tiny wedges served as a canapé may be eaten with the fingers.

PLANKED—Meat or fish on a wooden board broiled under a flame.

PLUMS—Hold fresh plums in fingers and eat as close to the pit as possible.

PORT WINE—Dry port wine is sometimes served in place of a cocktail. Sweet port wine is served as a dessert wine. Serve at room temperature or very slightly cooled.

POTATO CHIPS—Eat with the fingers. If served with a "dip" try not to leave slivers in the dip.

POTPOURRI (pot-poor-ree)—A mixture of highly seasoned meats.

RADISHES—Take from the relish dish, place on butter plate or dinner plate, and eat with the fingers. Take small bites.

RAGOÛT (rah-goo)—A thick savory stew.

RAVIOLI (rah-vee-oh'-lee)—An Italian dish. Small cases of thin noodle dough containing ground meat or cheese. Served with sauce and cheese. Eaten with a fork.

SALADS AND SALAD BOWL—Salads should be eaten with a fork. Knife is used only for cutting a wedge of lettuce. When salad is served in a large salad bowl, a large spoon and fork are provided for shifting the serving to your plate.

SALT—If dipping radishes or celery in salt, place the salt on the butter plate or the edge of the dinner plate, never on the table. If open salts are used and no salt spoon is provided, use a clean knife to take salt from a common container; if individual salts are used, take the salt with the fingers.

SAUTÉ (so-tay)—Fried quickly in small amount of fat.

SCONES—These are sweet biscuits. In England they are served with afternoon tea and are then eaten with the fingers. If served at luncheon they are eaten as any other hot bread.

SHERBET OR ICE—Eat with a spoon when served as a dessert. Never leave the spoon in the sherbet glass. Use a fork if the sherbet is served with the main course, as with turkey.

SHRIMP—Ordinarily eaten with a fork and may be cut into several bites. French fried with tails on, they are taken in the fingers by the tail, dipped in sauce, and eaten down to the tail. Small shrimp eaten cold with cocktails are taken in the fingers or on a toothpick.

SMORGASBORD—A Swedish-type of luncheon or supper surved buffet style. Consists of many hors d'oeuvres, hot and cold meats, smoked and pickled fish, cheese, sausages, salads, and desserts. It is correct to serve one's own plate from the buffet and to take as much or as little as one wishes. It is also correct to return to the buffet for repeat servings, as long as this is not overdone.

SNAILS—These are usually served on a hot metal platter. Hot snail shell is gripped with the holder, and the snail is extracted with a cocktail fork or pick and put whole into the mouth. Drink the juice from the shell.

SOUPS—May be drunk or taken with a spoon when served in a cup. The bouillon spoon is always placed in the saucer when not in use. Soup served in a large bowl or flat soup plate is taken with a large soup spoon, which is left in the soup plate when not in use. Never fill a soup spoon more than three-fourths full and always sip from the side of the spoon. It is permissible to tip the soup plate away from you when it is nearly empty.

SPAGHETTI—Try to master wrapping this around your fork, a few strands at a time. A spoon held in your left hand or the plate itself may be used as a barricade. Cut the spaghetti with your fork if you must, but not with your knife.

SUGAR—Cube or loaf sugar should be taken with the sugar tongs, but fingers may be used if necessary. Be sure to touch only the cube you are taking for yourself.

TABLE D'HÔTE (tah-bl-dote)—A fixed-price meal.

TIMBALE—A baked mold made of a variety of meat or vegetable combinations.

TORTE (tor′ta)—A rich, sticky cake, made with nuts, fruit, meringue.

VIN (van)—Wine.

WATERMELON—Usually cut into large wedges and eaten with a fork. Remove the seeds with the fork tines and cut pieces with the side of your fork.

WINE—See wine chart on page 83.

YORKSHIRE PUDDING—A popover-type pudding served with roast beef and the juices of the beef.

WINE AND LIQUOR CHART

TYPE OF DRINK	WHEN SERVED	WITH WHAT	TEMPERATURE	GLASS
Cocktails	before meals	canapés	iced	cocktail—well filled
Highballs— gin and tonic— whisky and soda	before meals or at cocktail parties	better alone	with ice	highball—well filled
Appetizer Wines dry sherry— dry vermouth	before dinner cocktail parties	canapés hors d'oeuvres nuts—cheese	chilled	all purpose wine glass ⅔-full
Red Table Wine chianti—claret— Burgundy—Rosé	during dinner	usually red meats— not fish highly seasoned foods	room temperature	all purpose wine glass ⅔-full
White Table Wine Sauterne—Moselle— Chablis	during dinner or luncheon	white meats such as chicken or fish	chilled	all purpose wine glass
Dessert Wines sherry—port— muscatel—tokay	with dessert	dessert or light refreshment	room temperature or slightly cool	all purpose wine glass or sherry glass
Sparkling Wine champagne— Burgundy	during any festive meal or other special occasion	main course, dessert, or light refreshment	chilled	6 oz. saucer glass or wine glass
Brandy—Liqueurs	after dinner with coffee		room temperature	liqueur glass or small brandy inhaler

83

The Frenchman . . . endeavors to do what there is to be done without superfluous . . . or fancy gestures. He sits down, ties his napkin behind his ears, picks up a knife and fork and goes to work with admirable directness. He dunks his bread in the juice of the snail, he chases fragments of steak and gravy with a piece of crust, he licks his fingers, says Ah! *and gets fed.*

—WESTBROOK PEGLER [1]

7

At Table:
Table Setting
and Service

Food is to eat—and enjoy! Thus far we will go with Mr. Pegler's Frenchman. The social situation of the dinner table is obviously of little consequence to this individual, whether he be French, English, Italian, or just plain American. *He* enjoyed his meal, but what about his table companions? To most readers of this book, the companionship of eating together is at least as important as is the character of the food being served. And companionship is always happiest when the physical environment is well under our control. At table this implies knowledge of tools and implements and the skill to use them, as well as of what we might call the geography of table service.

The illustrations on pages 84 and 91 picture objects commonly encountered on breakfast-luncheon-dinner-supper tables in the United States. Depending upon the circles in which you move, you may rarely come face to face with such items as the finger bowl, the cocktail fork, the after-dinner coffee cup, or the sherry glass. Society in our land and in our time is exceptionally fluid, however, and you never know when a new experience may overtake you. Even if you have only pictorial knowledge of some of these things, this is likely to stand you in good stead some day.

[1] From a Westbrook Pegler column. Used by permission, courtesy of Westbrook Pegler and Roy Howard.

A. PLACE SETTING FOR AN
INFORMAL DINNER

The geography of the table setting—what you see as you sit down to table—is pictured in the accompanying illustrations. Here you will see (A) a place setting for an informal dinner; (B) a place setting for luncheon—some of the dinner items may be missing, others changed for smaller or simpler versions; and (C) a place setting for a formal dinner. Buffet and tea service arrangements are pictured in the next chapter. All of these arrangements agree with the customary good usage of our time. They may be simplified or elaborated as necessity or special situation dictates without resulting in offense. In other words, these are not the *only* acceptable and correct table settings, but if you wish guidance in this area, these illustrations will serve your need.

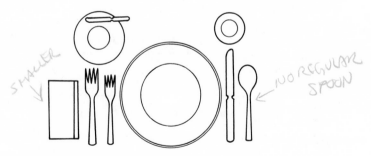

B. PLACE SETTING FOR A LUNCHEON

Illustrations alone cannot tell the whole story of good table service, however. Certain practical rules have been established to facilitate service and contribute to the enjoyment of guests, family, host, and hostess. The resourceful person adapts these rules to his or her own situation in order to express individuality and to achieve

c. Place Setting for a
Formal Dinner

novelty and interest, remembering only the dictates of good taste and the appeal of unostentatious simplicity; remembering also that a meal, like a work of art, is most successful when it has coherence, a theme, harmony.

Setting the Table

The dining table, for whatever meal, should be well-balanced, uncluttered, with plenty of elbow room for the comfort of family and guests. (See illustration D.)

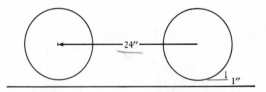

d. Spacing of Place Settings

THE TABLE COVER

A full-size *dinner cloth* is laid over a silence cloth or pad and is expected to overhang the edges of the table by from 10 to 15 inches. A very large table is improved in appearance if the drop is even greater than this. *Lace, voile,* or *net cloths* are placed directly over the table without a silence cloth—this in order to allow the gleaming wood of the table to show through. Casual dining and entertaining tends to get away from the large dinner cloth in favor of small color-ful _luncheon cloths_ or _table mats_. Especially for breakfast or luncheon these are quite appropriate, and for any but the really dressy dinner, formal-styled, often beautifully detailed table mats are quite in order.

THE CENTERPIECE

The centerpiece reflects the taste and imagination of the hostess and sets the theme of the occasion. A small decoration with simple lines is more attractive than one which crowds the table. A few flowers are often more effective than many. Colors should blend or harmonize or contrast artistically with the linen and china. Fruits are a colorful and attractive decoration when skillfully arranged in a bowl or on the table itself. In recent years vegetables have gained popularity as informal design pieces. The height of the centerpiece is very important. It should be low enough so that even the shortest person seated at table can see across the table (this means in effect not more than 12 inches high). For a buffet or tea table the centerpiece may be any height, since guests will not be seated and there will be no danger of obstructing the view.

CANDLELIGHT

The use of candles on the dinner table is optional. Many women dearly love them and many men dearly hate them. Candles are never used unless they are lighted. They are used only for dinner, after-noon teas, cocktail parties, and late suppers—never for breakfast or luncheon. Always use four or more candles in order to provide suffi-cient illumination, and make sure that they are tall enough to be out of the line of direct vision of those seated at table, as the flickering points of light can be very annoying.

SILVER OR STAINLESS FLATWARE

The _flatware_ (cutlery) necessary for a meal is a part of the place setting. (See illustrations A and B.) Use only the pieces necessary for the menu. Try not to use more than six pieces for each place setting. If additional silver is needed, it may be brought in when dessert and coffee are served. Place the implements with military precision one inch from the edge of the table and compactly enough to give an appearance of unity. As can be seen in the illustrations, the pieces are arranged for each course in order of use, starting from far left and far right and working in toward the plate.

Knives go to the right of the plate with *cutting edge toward the plate*. Do not include one unless it will be needed.

Forks go to the left of the plate with dinner fork on the outside, salad fork next, and possibly a dessert fork next to the plate. Or the dessert fork may be brought in later. If salad is served as a first course, then the salad fork will be at the far left with the dinner fork following. For a simple luncheon or dessert, when no knife is used, the fork may be placed to the right of the plate with the spoon next to it. The oyster or cocktail fork is placed to the extreme right of the spoons, or on the plate beside the cocktail. It is never placed to the left with the other forks.

Spoons, bowls up, are placed to the right of the knife. The soup or bouillon spoon would be on the extreme right if soup is to be the first course. One teaspoon is customary, for coffee or tea, unless a fruit cocktail or small-spoon dessert is contemplated, in which case two teaspoons should be placed. If an iced drink will replace the hot beverage, then an iced-tea spoon should replace one of the regular teaspoons. The large dessert spoon, or teaspoon for dessert, should be next to the knife. The demitasse spoon is never a part of the place setting. It should always be on the saucer when the demitasse is served.

E. PLACING OF SPREADERS ON
BREAD-AND-BUTTER PLATES

Butter spreaders are allowed more latitude of position than perhaps any other piece of flatware. They may be placed on, and to the rear of, the bread-and-butter plate, lying parallel to the edge of the table and with the handle to the right; or they may be placed on, and to the right-hand side of, the bread-and-butter plate, directly at right angles to the edge of the table; or they may be laid diagonally across the bread-and-butter plate. (See illustration E.) If the bread-and-butter plate is omitted, as for breakfast, then the spreader may be placed above the breakfast plate, parallel with the edge of the table.

Serving pieces are placed on the table in front of the host or hostess who will serve. They are never brought to table already placed in the dish to be distributed. The carving knife is placed to the right of the meat platter, the carving fork to the left. Serving implements for other dishes are placed beside the host's or hostess's own silver. Spoons and forks, for serving jams, relishes, or other condiments may be placed alongside the dish they are to accompany.

CHINA, POTTERY, OR PLASTICWARE

The dinner, luncheon, or breakfast plate takes its place, like the flatware, one inch from the table's edge. The *service plate*—a teaser from the formal days of our now-ancient history—has little practical significance today except as a base for a soup plate or bowl, or perhaps for a casserole. If used, it also would be placed one inch from the table edge.

The bread-and-butter plate belongs directly above the tip of the dinner fork. Should space be at a premium, a butter pat can be substituted for the bread-and-butter plate, in which case it would occupy the spot above the fork. Use of a butter knife would probably be omitted in this situation as there would be no suitable place for laying it down after use. At a truly formal dinner, or whenever the hostess so desires, butter will not be served and there will be no bread-and-butter plate, no butter pat, and no butter spreader. The rolls, biscuits, or bread will be served already buttered and may be laid directly on the cloth for convenience.

The salad plate belongs to the left of the forks one inch from the edge of the table.

Side dishes, usually of heavily sauced vegetables, are placed wherever symmetry and room permit. Formally, they are never used, but informally they may be used and must be taken into consideration in your table arrangement. Side dishes are not used as often as in the past.

GLASSES

The types of glasses most commonly encountered are shown in illustration F. Glasses are placed above the knife and to the right of the place setting. (See illustration C.)

The water glass (tumbler or goblet) is always placed above the tip of the dinner knife.

Fruit juice or vegetable (tomato) juice glasses would be presented as a course in themselves and would usually be placed on their own plate in the center of the place setting. Informally they may be placed next to, and to the right of, the water glass, allowing the main breakfast or luncheon plate to be in place at the beginning of the meal.

Cocktail   Tall water   Red wine
           goblet

Sherry   Hollow stem   Low sherbet
      champagne   and white wine

Cordial   Highball   Old fashioned
or liqueur   (13 ounce)

F. Common Types of Drinking Glasses

Wine glasses, if used, are placed above the spoons in a straight line diagonally directed toward the edge of the table. The glass to be removed first would be the nearest to the right. Wine service presents an area of etiquette in which the unwary may easily swim out too far and drown. For most of us, here, simplicity is to be emphasized. Remember that, for most purposes, wine is served in very small quantities (two to four ounces) and it is attractive in delicate glasses suited to hold this quantity. (See illustration C.)

ACCESSORIES

Napkins are folded into a square or rectangle (avoid fancy shapes). They may be laid on the service plate if one is used but more often are placed to the left of the fork with open edge either to the left or the right. Since most people are right-handed, it is more convenient to put the fold at the outside edge of the place setting. For ordinary American family service it is probable that the use of paper napkins has become more the rule than the exception. They may appear, as well, at cocktail parties and at informal suppers. When used, they should be of good quality and should be handled in the same way as the still more correct linen napkin.

Individual sets of salt and pepper are placed above the plate or between, and above, each two place settings.

G. The Finger Bowl Is Brought in on the Dessert Plate, and Is Removed to Leave the Dessert Plate Free.

Ash trays are placed directly above each plate or between each two place settings.

Place cards belong on the folded napkin or in clear view above the dinner plate: "Mr. Nall" or "Mrs. Nall"—avoid first names.

Finger bowls, if used, may be placed after the dessert plate is removed, or they may be brought in on the dessert plate before the dessert is served. In this case the dessert fork and spoon appear on either side of the bowl. Using both hands, remove the finger bowl and place it above the dessert plate for use at the end of the meal. The fork is then removed from the plate to the left and the spoon to the right, leaving a clear plate for receiving the dessert. (See illustration G.)

THE HUMAN ELEMENT

Having familiarized ourselves with the layout of the dining table, let us take a look at the human element that sits facing the place settings at table.

First of all, the seating arrangements are the result of ancient and well-established tradition. The host sits at one end of the table; the hostess sits opposite him at the head of the table; the lady guest of honor sits to the right of the host; the male guest of honor sits to the right of the hostess; the remaining guests and family are seated according to the direction of the hostess. A diagram of such a setting arrangement appears on page 54. Ordinarily, the hostess endeavors to avoid seating two women or two men next to each other, but practically this is often almost impossible. If it is of sufficient importance to her, the hostess herself may move to the left side of the table and seat the male guest of honor in her usual position at the head of the table, thus achieving an evenly mixed group. When possible, do not seat husbands and wives next to each other or immediately across the table from each other. Unmarried couples are quite properly seated thus. (See also seating diagrams for restaurant dining on page 54.) Place cards can, of course, be used to simplify seating arrangements, but for parties of eight or fewer they are rarely used.

To simplify service, the bread or rolls, butter, relish tray or dishes, salad course, and filled water glass (chilled, we hope) should be in place before the group is seated. If the first course is a very hot soup or a chilled dish, it may also be in place. A dish requiring fresh-from-the-stove service to be at its best should be served after the seating has taken place and while the guests are arranging their napkins and adjusting themselves to the table.

If the main course is going to require carving at table, this is the host's job, and he may also be expected to serve the vegetables. To expedite matters and see that the food arrives at the guests' plates hot and tempting, a daughter of the house, some other relative or good friend, or the hostess herself may assist with this chore. The host serves the guest to his right first and so on around the table, without regard to "ladies first" or other precedence concerns. As mentioned in a previous chapter, other dishes on the table are started by persons near them and are passed always to the right. You accept the dish with your right hand, transfer it to your left hand while using your right hand again to serve yourself, then continue the dish on its travels to the right—always passing in one direction. Each person at table should be alert to the needs of others, passing rolls, butter, etc., when someone else is ready for them. Particularly remember to pass cream and sugar for coffee after this is served, even though you yourself may not care for them.

When everyone has finished eating, the dishes are removed, starting with the guest of honor. From the left, pick up the dinner plate, transfer it to the right hand, then lift the bread-and-butter plate. Repeat until all places have been cleared. Never use a tray or attempt to remove too much at one time. If the kitchen is at some distance, however, a rolling serving table, inconspicuously placed, may be used.

All food, with the exception of beverages, is served and removed from the left of the seated diner. Beverages are served and removed from the right. If some awkward situation makes it more convenient, however, it is perfectly acceptable to modify this rule as the situation indicates. Smoothness and speed of service should determine your choice of method. When necessary to do so, refill water and wine glasses, as well as tea and coffee cups, from the right and without lifting from the table.

Salt and pepper shakers, extra dishes, and all extra silver should be removed from the table before dessert is served. The table is crumbed with a folded napkin and tray, or with one of the many devices now available for this purpose.

If food is being served by a maid, waiter, or other helper, it will be offered to you from your left, so wait until the dish appears at your left before helping yourself.

A hostess should pace her eating so as not to finish before her slowest guest. This is to save slow-eating guests embarrassment.

If guests are late, traditionally a hostess need delay only fifteen minutes before announcing the meal. To wait longer than twenty minutes may show lack of consideration for hungry guests who arrived on time. A guest arriving after a meal has started goes directly to the hostess to offer an apology, then starts the meal at whatever stage the other guests have reached.

Technique and Tradition

Since most of us, by the time we are able to read this book, have been feeding ourselves with a fair amount of success since perhaps sometime in the first year of life, it may come as a jolt to be told that what we have been doing is possibly all wrong. True, we have conveyed food from a dish into our mouth and hence have sustained life—but at what cost to the raw nerves of our families and table companions?

Perhaps we have not, like Mr. Pegler's Frenchman, taken "food as it comes, without false restrictions on style or stance, and . . . (made our) victuals holler 'Uncle!' " But perhaps we *have* been in the habit of gripping our fork as we did at the winsome age of two in our tight and now not so little fist and coming at our mouth with the graceful agility of a steam-shovel. Let's check-up and, if necessary, correct-up!

HOW DO YOU USE YOUR SILVERWARE?

The most noticeable technique problems lie in the area of table cutlery usage.

Begin eating with the first implement at the far left of your place setting or with the one at the far right, depending upon the dish placed in front of you. If this is a seafood cocktail or oysters on the half-shell, use the cocktail fork which you will find at the extreme right of the spoons. If your first course is a cup soup, a clear bouillon or bisque, there will be no cocktail fork and your first implement to the far right, which you will use, will be a bouillon spoon, a soup-dessert spoon, or even a plain teaspoon. This spoon you dip *away* from you and sip the liquid, noiselessly we hope, from the side of the spoon—not the front. Or, if you prefer, lift the cup by the handle and, in leisurely sips, drink the contents. If your first course is a plate (or bowl) soup, the implement you will use, and the implement that will be placed at the far right ready for your use, will be a tablespoon-size soup spoon. Soup thus served usually contains bits of vegetable-meat-pasta which can be more readily captured in a large spoon. Sipping, under these circumstances, is hardly practicable, but you don't need to swallow the spoon along with the liquid. Manipulate this spoon as you find necessary in the circumstances but do it noiselessly and unostentatiously. It is perfectly good form to tip a soup plate—away from you—for a final one or two spoonfuls.

If the first course you encounter is a fruit cocktail, you will use the first spoon you find at the far right of your place setting. This will probably be a teaspoon; or if a half grapefruit, or even a half orange, is served, the spoon provided may be a sharp-pointed orange spoon. Should a sectioned melon appear instead of the other foods mentioned, once again use the teaspoon at the far right of your place setting. Occasionally a salad—or an Italian antipasto—is served as a luncheon or dinner lead course. In this case you will find a salad fork first in rank on the far left of your place setting and this is the implement to use.

It is when the main course—the meat course—of the meal arrives that your cutlery manners may begin to show. How do you hold your knife and fork while cutting your meat? What do you do with the knife after cutting? How many bites do you cut at once? What do you do with both knife and fork when passing your plate for seconds? or when you wish to indicate that you are finished with your plate? The following pointers may reassure you that you are doing these things according to present-day good form, or they may be timely alerts to some irritating bad habit.

Somewhere in the not-too-clear background of American history, when our colonial forefathers cut the apron strings that held them to Europe, they staged a revolution in knife-and-fork manners as well as in politics. Looking at it today, it seems as if they did it the hard way, because our meat-cutting routine is more involved than is that of our cousins across the sea. Europeans regard us as indulging in sheer waste motion, but we are not entirely without reason on our side. Let us look at the distinctions.

American-style knife-and-fork routine. Hold the fork in your left hand, prongs down and firmly planted in the food you are cutting.

Your left index finger should extend in a straight line down the handle, but it should not touch the prongs. Hold the knife in your right hand, index finger extended sufficiently to apply whatever pressure is necessary. Cut with the knife on the *outside* of the fork. (See illustration H). Never mistake your fork for a spear and grip it midway down the handle, forcing it to stand at right angles to the plate, upright, like a standard in the midst of the battlefield of your plate. (See illustrations I, K, L.) When your bite is cut—*one* bite, or at most *two*—lay your knife on the edge of the plate, switch your fork to the right hand and, *prongs up,* eat! (See illustration M.) This routine has the advantage that you are using your skillful right hand at all times for the techniques which require skill. This is not true of the so-called English or European method.

European-style knife-and-fork routine. Hold the fork in your left hand and the knife in your right in the same manner as is described above. Cut your bite—but now, instead of shifting hands with the fork, simply convey the food to your mouth with left hand, using the fork *prongs down* as it was in the cutting. (See illustration N.) You may lay the knife down while you do this, or if your table companions understand that this is the continental manner, you may use your knife as a pusher. This routine, we feel sure, would have the endorsement of Mr. Pegler's Frenchman, because it imposes fewer obstacles between his mouth and the food. When you are using this routine, however, it is important to remember to stop at intervals, lay the knife and fork down, relax, chat a bit. Otherwise this highly efficient eating system will have your plate clean with embarrassing rapidity.

When passing your plate for seconds, lay the knife and fork close together near the center of the plate, fork tines up and near the center, knife with sharp edge next to the fork and at right. (See illustration O.)

When finished eating, lay the knife and fork close together with the fork on the left, tines up, knife on the right with cutting edge facing the fork. (See illustration P.) Never rest any piece of silver an angle, part on and part off the plate.

Serving spoons, large serving forks, or both will accompany food offered on a platter, in a salad bowl, or in a serving dish. If these are presented to you by waiter or hostess-assistant, he or she will appear at your left and will hold the dish while you help yourself. "Spoon food" such as peas presents no problem. With your right hand you help yourself to a reasonable portion and replace the spoon. A leafy salad or slippery meat or vegetable dish will be accompanied by both serving spoon and fork. Take the spoon in your right hand and the fork in your left, slip the spoon under the food and hold it in place with the fork while you transfer the serving to your plate. If the serving dish is passed around the table without benefit of waiter, it is courteous to hold the dish for one's neighbor while the serving is accomplished.

The *salad fork*, if provided, is always used for eating the salad, whether this is a separate course or is served as part of the main course. If there is salad, but no salad fork, use your dinner fork.

Avoid leaving spoons where they can easily be knocked out of a dish. After using, they are usually laid on the saucer or plate upon which the fruit cocktail, sherbet, or whatever has been served. When sodas or tall drinks are served, there may be no choice but to leave the spoon in the glass, although this is awkward. *Never* leave coffee or teaspoons in the cup. If open salt dishes are used, the little salt spoons remain in the dish. Should individual open salt dishes be used without the little spoons, you may pinch out some of the salt with your fingers, or you may use the tip of a clean knife.

STEMWARE, COFFEE CUPS, AND FINGER BOWLS

Goblets and stemmed juice and wine glasses are held between thumb and fingers at the top of the stem and the bottom of the bowl. Avoid spreading your hand around the flared top, and handle these items with care as sometimes they are very delicate. (See illustration Q.)

Hold the coffee or tea cup with handle between your thumb and fingers. Do not hook a finger through the handle. Avoid any appearance of affectation by keeping the fingers close together. (See illustration R.)

Finger bowls are a great convenience and are simple to use. Dip the tips of the fingers of one hand at a time and dry them on your napkin, which is held in your lap. You may touch your moistened fingers to your lips, but don't moisten the napkin for this purpose.

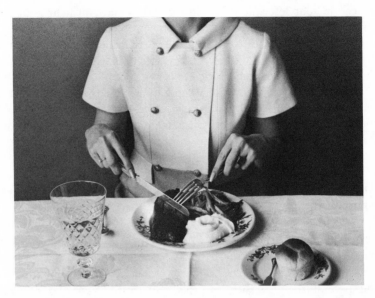

H. The Correct Way to Cut Meat

I. An Incorrect Way to Cut Meat

J. An Incorrect Way to Cut Meat

K. An Incorrect Way to Cut Meat

L. An Incorrect Way to Cut Meat

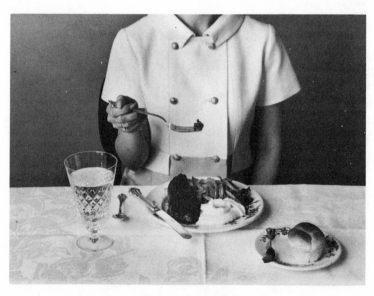

M. The Correct Way to Convey Food to
the Mouth (American Style)

N. THE CORRECT WAY TO CONVEY FOOD TO THE MOUTH
(EUROPEAN STYLE)

O. PASSING THE PLATE FOR SECONDS

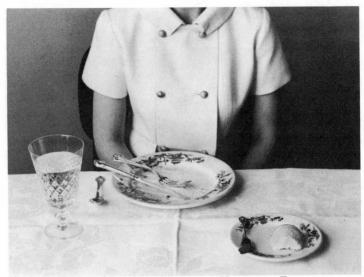

P. THE POSITION OF THE KNIFE AND FORK
AT THE END OF THE MEAL

Q. THE CORRECT WAY TO HOLD A GOBLET

R. The Correct Way to Hold a Tea Cup or
Coffee Cup

8

At Table: The Lighter Side

Except for the food itself, the *sine qua non* of meal service for whatever occasion is the table. The family dog and cat unprotestingly take their meals from dishes set on the floor, but, baby to octogenarian, we humans like to find our food raised on some sort of pedestal. This may be as low as those traditional to the Japanese culture (perhaps no more than six inches from the floor), or as high as the stand-up eating counters sometimes found in our urban quick-lunch restaurants—but tables, a place to lay our food, we must have.

Tables are not necessarily for sitting at; they may be for standing around; or they may be simply a base of operations to which we go for supplies and renewals in the numerous informal eating situations dear to the hearts of party-loving and efficiency-minded Americans.

In the previous two chapters we have described social situations and suggested procedures applicable to commonly encountered eating situations. Most of the prescribed manners are equally mandatory whether one is dining formally with the president of one's company or enjoying a backyard barbecue at the home of a long-time and intimate friend. Table manners are built-in personality characteristics, and they will serve you well or ill regardless of the nature of the

104

social situation. Off-the-table service does present its own unique problems, however, and these we intend to discuss in this chapter.

THE TEA OR COFFEE HOUR

Afternoon tea, a phrase and a rite borrowed from our English cousins, is a charming custom. "There are few hours in life more agreeable than the hour dedicated to the ceremony known as afternoon tea," wrote Henry James, and there are many people on both sides of the Atlantic who still concur in this opinion. The term *afternoon tea* has by extension come to include the serving of coffee, chocolate, or even soft or hard drinks. It is a more nearly formalized ceremony than are any of the other services we intend to describe here. Having a long tradition in polite society, it *can* be an excessively precise routine, its all-too-obvious purpose being scarcely more than the paying off of social debts. Large teas call for conventional service and careful planning, lest they disintegrate in confusion. They *can* be friendly, however, and when they are characterized by warmth and kindness, they are a very pleasant way for both old friends and strangers to meet and chat. Small teas, served to a few neighbors or good friends, are well-known as intimate, happy occasions. A few suggestions here may be useful for hostesses planning either type of tea.

Being an afternoon affair, the tea party is traditionally, and in fact largely, feminine in atmosphere. This is by no means entirely so, however. In university, art, music, or literary circles there may be a large proportion of men attending, and the masculine interest should never be ignored when this is the case. In other words, if you are serving delicate little sandwiches and cakes, at least have plenty of them and be prepared to offer coffee if your male guest eyes the teacups gloomily.

At a tea having more than a very few guests, the hostess may choose to use her dining room table for the service. She uses her ingenuity in creating a beautiful and imaginative setting, perhaps laying out her best linen, china, crystal, and silver, or perhaps seeking a more colorful homespun effect by use of simple brass and pottery. She must execute every detail with care to avoid a cluttered look. The teacups, on their saucers and *not* stacked, should be arranged as

TABLE FOR AN AFTERNOON TEA

close as possible to the tea service so the person pouring will not
have to reach out for them. A plate of lemon slices, with lemon fork,
should be near, as should the milk pitcher, a cream pitcher if coffee
is being served, and sugar bowl containing preferably small lump

sugar and complete with sugar tongs. Spoons, napkins, and plates, if the refreshment will require these, should be arranged in a unit. Refreshments for very large teas should preferably be finger foods—sandwiches, small cakes or cookies, or perhaps tiny pastries. If more elaborate refreshments are desired, these should be arranged on their plates and laid on the table, with necessary fork or spoon already on the plate beside them.

Tea, coffee, or chocolate should be kept hot—the many varieties of warming devices now available are useful here. Hot water for diluting the tea should also always be at hand in a separate pot. Cold drinks such as punch or iced tea are also sometimes served and must be kept cold. In this case, glasses and tall-drink spoons are substituted for the cups, saucers, and teaspoons.

Serving can be relatively easy. At a large tea, friends of the hostess will have been asked in advance to pour. The hostess herself will be busy greeting and introducing guests and overseeing the service. The ladies who are serving will be seated at the table, one for each service. Sometimes several tea services will be set at the big table or several small tables provided. The guests come to the table to be served and carry away their cup, saucer, teaspoon, and sandwiches and cookies or separate small plate of the refreshment. The tea-pouring friend asks each guest whether she will have tea, coffee, lemon, cream or milk, sugar. Napkins will be available either on the refreshment plate or near the sandwich and cookie serving plates. The guests find small tables, book shelves, chair arms, or any convenient spot for laying down their dishes, and, in congenial groups, enjoy their tea. Most desirably, each guest should come to the table to serve herself; taking the refreshments around, as is sometimes done, deprives the guest of enjoying the table and of selecting her own food.

A maid, if there is one, or a friend or relative may assist the hostess in keeping the table supplied with tea, coffee, fresh cups and saucers or glasses, and sees to it that the sandwich and cake trays, as well as cream pitchers and so forth, are kept filled. When partially empty, these should be removed as fresh ones are brought in, making it possible for the last guest coming to table to find it just as attractive as the first one found it.

At a small, intimate tea, the hostess will probably use an attractively arranged little table in the living room and will take care of the pouring and refreshment-serving herself. Several small tables may be more convenient and attractive in this situation than an overcrowded single table. When only a few guests are present, it is usually possible to supply them with individual stack tables for their cups, saucers, and plates—an aspect of the small tea which makes it a particularly satisfying experience.

Hostesses sometimes, with a limited group, set up either one large table or several small ones with place settings in very much the same fashion as for luncheon. This may add to the comfort of guests, but some of the characteristic atmosphere of the tea hour is sacrificed. There is no objection to tea being served in this fashion, although standing around, rather than sitting down at a tea seems more conducive to good talking and the making of new friends.

The Cocktail Party

Paralleling the afternoon tea in some respects and the buffet supper in others, the cocktail party seems to have become the United States' contribution to leisurely and informal entertaining. Usually held later in the day than the afternoon tea, the cocktail party lends itself more readily to mixed-group activity. In its perhaps most frequent form it is an after-work and before-dinner period of relaxation, although it may often include a buffet supper of sufficient proportions to make a later dinner undesirable.

In theory the cocktail party is an almost ideal solution to many entertainment headaches, but in practical fact it carries with it a heavy load of its own special problems. There is, for instance, the time problem. Guests are invited for cocktails from five to seven in the evening. But how often guests are still present, sometimes in numbers, at eleven P.M.!

Just because some gluttonous people have been known to eat themselves to death, we do not forego the dinner party. Similarly, just because some people do not control their drinking habits, we do not condemn all cocktail parties. We do, however, emphatically refrain from inviting such people to our cocktail parties when this is possible. We scrupulously abide by the "new regulation" added to "the present rules of etiquette" by three Rutgers University sociologists: "Never insist on anyone taking a drink." And we always provide interesting and delicious nonalcoholic beverages for people who, for whatever reason, do not wish to take alcohol. These may be in the form of a milk drink, a fruit punch, tomato juice, or any of the ubiquitous bottled soft drinks preferred by many people. The soft drinks should be as easily and unostentatiously available as the cocktails, and neither hosts nor courteous guests should show any surprise or even awareness of a guest's choice of drinks.

Cocktail parties are, obviously, not suitable entertainment for groups of under-legal-age guests. Probably few young people today reach maturity, however, without finding themselves present, knowingly or unwittingly, at a cocktail party. Knowledge lends strength in this area as well as in any other area of social relationship. The young man or woman must know what to expect in order to determine his own attitude and conduct.

Drinks for the cocktail party may be mixed in the kitchen and brought in to the party on trays. This is customary when servants or a catering service are employed for the occasion. It may also be the best solution when the host and one or two friends are officiating as drink-mixers. In this way the drinking may be slowly paced. The playroom or living room bar is a not-easily-discouraged attraction when one is available, however. When a bar is set up, the host, a friend, or a hired bartender serves the drinks, and the guests approach the bar when they are ready.

The buffet served at a cocktail party can be one of its most attractive features. There is almost nothing from soups to desserts that can be considered out of place as food at a cocktail party. Hors d'oeuvres of every conceivable sort are acceptable as well as hot or cold soups, hot or cold casseroles, hot or cold roasts, any and all types of bread and rolls, relishes, and salads. Only the rich desserts—ice cream, cake, pie—may be a little unusual, but even these are sometimes served, and there is usually a sweet of some description. Coffee must be kept practically on tap, with tea or caffeine-free coffee available on request. The buffet service for cocktail parties is the same in its essentials as the self-service buffet described in the next section. Guests rarely sit at tables for these parties, although there is no objection to the use of the little stack tables as long as they do not impede the free movement of guests through the party area.

Cocktails before dinner (when the invitation has been to dinner) are not to be mistaken for a cocktail party. In this case the cocktails are incidental to the dinner. They are usually made in the kitchen and brought into the living room on a tray. One or two are the limit before sitting down to table, and the hors d'oeuvres served with them are very limited in variety—perhaps nothing more than some tasty little crackers or cocktail tidbits.

BUFFET MEALS

The cartoonist Leo Garel once pictured a party-dressed couple approaching the closed door of a friend's house. Incongruously, the well-dressed man is carrying with him a small table. The wife, in addition to her mink coat, is wearing a disapproving look. The caption reads, "I don't care what they think. I'm through with juggling plates at these buffet suppers." Few of us will fail to feel a keen sympathy for this cartoon man. Like him, we have been faced with almost superhuman balancing acts, and not a few of us have ended up, like Fido, eating from a dish on the floor. The moral of our story is this: when serving a buffet meal, if seating at a table has not been contemplated, provide in so far as you possibly can small tables, stools, chairs, hassocks, shelves—*some* cleared space that will hold a plate, glass, and cup and saucer. If the floor must be used (and for young people this is really no great drawback), provide trays or, at the very least, place mats. Place mats (the paper ones are excellent) are a wise addition in any event, as a protection for fine furniture.

Buffet meals have become a highly popular form of entertaining. They are the answer to entertaining a group of almost any number of guests and can be undertaken in the smallest apartment or the most spacious home. Kitchen help and maid service are hard to come by and expensive and can be curtailed or eliminated in the simplified service of the buffet. The buffet meal may be as casual or elaborate, and the group to be entertained may be as large or as small as the party-giver desires and the situation permits. The buffet meal also means less strain on both host and hostess and allows them to enjoy the party along with their guests.

A further asset for the buffet meal, from the party-giver's point of view, is that it allows an almost unlimited field for originality. Imagination in the choice of menu and decorative and service appointments is expected—always remember, however, that a party out of character with the house, the family circumstances, and the occasion is automatically doomed to failure. Good taste and suitability rule here as elsewhere in the area of etiquette. Order and planning there must be, else chaos will result. Thoughtful, imaginative, preplanned buffet entertaining may well create an atmosphere and occasion that your friends will long remember.

THE TABLE

Of course, in spite of the cartoon and the jokes, there *is* a buffet table, and sometimes there is a roomful of tables. The main table will be the dining table—perhaps pushed to the end of the room—or it may be a temporary structure of planks and table legs, or even wooden horses. The latter solution can provide the very long, narrow surface useful in buffet service—but take care that it is very solid and secure. The devastation of a collapsed buffet table is too terrible to contemplate. Whatever is used to provide the table, it is the table that sets the tone of the party. "First flowers then food on the table," says an old Danish proverb. The clever hostess chooses flowers for her table to complement her china and line. As on the dinner table, a few well-arranged flowers are more effective than many that give a crowded appearance.

Soft, gleaming candlelight (if this is an evening affair), shining silver, crystal, and fine linen may be used when the occasion is a real celebration—a silver or golden wedding anniversary, for instance, or an engagement announcement. Or, at the other extreme, a colored peasant cloth, wooden bowls, pottery dishes, copper or brass accessories, are quite in order and are to be preferred for breakfast, luncheon, or supper parties of the casual and probably more frequent get-together variety. Table mats may be used (except, need we say, on the plank-table described above) and are useful and attractive if care is taken to avoid a spotty effect; or the table may be left bare to set off its beautiful wood, if care is taken to protect it where dishes are placed on its surface. Should international dishes—on-the-table cooking of the Japanese sukiyaki, for instance—be part of the plan, the decor and theme of the party could include other aspects of that nation's life and cuisine. In other words, your party can and should have a theme, and the background and appointments should be in keeping with it.

In addition to the main table, small tables are often set in dining room, living room, hall, porch, wherever space is available. They may

EASTER TABLE WITH A TOUCH OF WHIMSEY

TABLE FOR AN INFORMAL BUFFET

112

simply be laid with cloth, or mats, and the guest acquires his necessary cutlery and napkin along with his food from the main table, or they may be set with regular place settings, and the guest goes to the main table only for actual food service. The small tables should harmonize in decoration with the main table and may even have their own centerpieces.

TYPES OF BUFFET SERVICE

The type of buffet service you choose for your party depends upon the number of people you invite, the help available, and the amount of room for entertainment. The food may be offered almost completely self-served or it may be almost completely waiter-served. Let us consider each type briefly.

The almost completely self-service arrangement is perhaps most often used for Sunday suppers, after-theater supper, special breakfasts, cocktail parties, large teas. It is quite suitable for entertaining a few friends and neighbors, and it may be an almost necessary choice if the occasion is a very populous one—perhaps a club affair—when any sort of small table use or serving through the crowd is almost out of the question. Organize the main table carefully in this situation to avoid the "subway rush" impression. Each guest helps himself to a plate, food, silver, napkin, and beverage. Then he is "on his own" so far as his eating accommodations and companions are concerned. When he wishes seconds, he returns to the buffet table of his own accord. The successful host and hostess keep an eye out for the lone wanderers in the crowd and try to attach them to each other or to some already-formed group.

What we might call semi-formal, or semi-self-service, buffet is perhaps the most often encountered. This includes provision of small tables, either completely or partially set for service, as described above. The guest takes his plate of food and possibly his cutlery from the main table to a small table. The host or hostess or a friend may serve one of the principal dishes at the buffet table, or the guests may be left to help themselves. The guests may likewise pour their own beverage; someone may be stationed at the table to pour it; or the hostess, maid, or friend may carry the serving pitcher or pot around to the small tables where cups or glasses have previously been placed.

When the guests have eaten, the hostess may choose to remove the used plates and serve the dessert directly to her guests at their tables, or the guests may be expected to return to the buffet table to obtain their dessert when they are ready for it. In the latter situation, good organization would require that some system of collecting the used dishes should be arranged for esthetic, as well as space, reasons.

The third system of buffet service is seldom seen outside of restaurants or hotels. In this situation you will always have a place at table provided for you. You will go to the well-staffed buffet table and indicate to the waiter what dishes you would like. He will serve you and most probably will circulate through the room later offering seconds, extra breads, relishes, beverage—the waiter always serves the beverage in this case, usually after you are seated in your place.

HINTS FOR SERVING YOUR BUFFET MEAL THE EASY WAY

1. Careful planning avoids last-minute rush. Success will depend, ultimately, upon how well you have foreseen and arranged the innumerable details.

2. Set the buffet table in logical order, having accessibility in mind. Your guests must be able to reach the serving dishes easily. Each dish should have beside it the necessary serving pieces—a salad spoon and fork with each salad bowl; a carving knife and fork near the ham or turkey, as well as the gravy or sauce if this is to be used. Salad dressing and ladle, if needed, should be near the salad; cream and sugar near the coffee.

3. Remember that it is difficult or impossible to use a knife for cutting meat on a plate held in your lap. Keep the relationship of menu to type of service in mind.

4. Be sure to have salt and pepper on the buffet table and possibly also on the small tables.

5. Use plates that are large enough to hold the offered foods without unsightly crowding. It is better to plan a few good dishes than to crowd the plate with many.

6. A stack of trays is a welcome sight to most guests if small tables are not available. This is especially true for supper, breakfast, and garden-terrace service. Men will nearly always prefer tables if these are at all possible, however.

7. It is helpful, whenever possible, to plan a menu that can be largely prepared a day in advance.

8. Hot dishes should be kept hot and grouped together. Table cooking is helpful. Use chafing dishes, electric cook pans, or even the Japanese charcoal *hibachis*. Electric or candle grilles and warmers can be used also. Cold dishes, likewise, should be grouped together in their own section of the buffet table.

9. Breads, rolls, biscuits, should be served buttered and ready to eat. If they are passed through the crowd, this should be done often.

10. Water, coffee, or any other beverage should be served from separate tables or a tea table if necessary to avoid a crowded appearance on the buffet table. Always aim for uncluttered simplicity. Arrange things, in so far as you can, in orderly rows. Have copious quantities of coffee available throughout the meal.

The Barbecue

A chapter on American informal meal service can no longer be considered complete unless it takes note of what we have come to call the barbecue. The barbecue is our latest and happiest excursion into outdoor dining. It may take place in some distinguished garden featuring full table service, uniformed chef and waiters, and an outdoor fireplace equipped with every usable gadget devised by the twentieth century; it may take place on some flagstoned terrace to the rear or side of the house—an area which may or may not be landscaped, shaded with an awning, screened, and set up more or less permanently with outdoor furniture, and which will have either a fireplace or a movable charcoal grille as its center of interest when mealtime comes around. It may also simply take place in the backyard, with a log fire in a crude stone fireplace or temporary grille as its center of action. Wherever it is and whatever its degree of elegance, the barbecue has become part of our culture. In the summer, America moves outdoors.

Meal service suggestions already given for buffet service most nearly cover the social situations encountered in outdoor eating. Tables are possibly even more important here than in indoor eating. Naturally one does not bring outdoors one's best linen, china, crystal, or silverware. Paper plates, cloths, and napkins are entirely adequate. Or plasticware may be an even better choice. The food table should most usefully be set up near the grille or fireplace. If the host enjoys the role of outdoor chef—and most men do—your main dish will be some meat lending itself to charcoal broiling. Unless sturdy tables and steak knives are provided, the easiest and probably neatest method of serving and consuming barbecued meat is in sandwich form. Should the portions be very large, a wooden board and heavy knife should be on hand for cutting the portions in halves or quarters before service. Also available in quantity should be paper napkins, salt and pepper, relishes, coffee, soda, or other beverage.

Preplanning for the outdoor meal is most important. Problems peculiar to this service are the weather, distance of eating area from kitchen, darkness, and insects. It is a wise host and hostess who never plan a barbecue which cannot be moved indoors promptly if weather conditions require it. Distance from the kitchen can be made less wearing by use of a wheeled serving cart. Some success with insect control has been achieved by prespraying of lawn and shrubbery—and incidentally, shrubbery harbors insects, so you may be less troubled if you set up your eating arrangements as much as possible in the open. Some twilight lamps are on the market which claim to not only provide after-dark illumination but also insect control. People who take their outdoor entertaining seriously should keep a constant check on new developments. Science, it seems apropros to remark, is wonderful.

Several other suggestions concerning outdoor dining may be mentioned here:

1. Remember the neighbors. They may not be able to see your party through the shrubbery, but they cannot escape its noise. Be considerate and keep your voices at least normally subdued.

2. If you are a guest at a barbecue, respect your host's gardens. A carelessly placed foot may crush some prized seedling. Do not pick flowers, break off tree branches, or dig holes in the turf. Do not scatter cigarette butts, napkins, tissues, or other debris over the yard any more than you would do this as a guest in the house. Being an outdoor guest tends to produce a free-wheeling, heady effect, but your manners are just as important here as at an indoor party.

Pleasantest of all ties is the tie of host and guest.

—AESCHYLUS

9

Hospitality: Host, Hostess, Guest

Successful entertaining is the result of a happy interaction among host, hostess, and guest, no one of whom can be considered without the others. A sense of appreciation and responsibility of one toward the other is essential. The chances are that the efforts of the hostess alone will not be enough unless her husband, the host, gives her full support. And the gracious host and hostess with a flair for details in entertaining may fail if the guest does not enter into the entertainment with enthusiasm. Usually the ideal guest is also an ideal host or hostess—the principles involved are the same for both roles. Consideration for others and forgetfulness of self are all-important.

The essence of successful entertaining is warm hospitality, and the basic rule is that it must be friendly and sincere with no attempt at pretense. Do the best that you can with what you have, and do not apologize.

Hospitality as an aspect of human relationships is probably as old as the human race. Every culture has had to deal with the guest situation and most cultures have conceded the guest a very privileged position. Many of our most cherished traditions have evolved around the hospitality relationship. What, then, do we mean by hospitality? What does hospitality imply?

Hospitality, as a social situation, exists whenever one person, the *guest*, entrusts himself or herself to the social control of another person or persons, the *host* and *hostess*. It may be as casual a situation as that of an invitation to "have a soda while we talk," issued by one of two friends who meet by chance on the street; or it may be an elaborate and long-anticipated party involving devoted and detailed planning.

Hospitality implies the *responsibility of host and hostess* to subordinate their own comfort and pleasure to the well-being and entertainment of the guest. The guest may be present as the result of their invitation, or he or she may be present at his own initiative—a routine call—or the situation may exist as a result of some occurrence beyond the control of any of the participants. The result is the same: host and hostess are socially responsible in every sense of the phrase for and to their guest.

Hospitality implies also the *responsibility of the guest* to respect his host's property, to conform with (and perhaps assist in) his host's plans, and to subordinate his personal preferences to the general desire. Having accepted hospitality, the guest is no longer a completely free agent. He is in the pleasantly anomalous situation of being at the same time in fee to his host and hostess, and the privileged individual whose comfort and entertainment they are bound to promote.

This responsibility code, although basic in most cultures, differs radically in its social expression among nations, economic groups, races, occupational groups—wherever differing group pressures exist. Within our own country, hospitality patterns show many sectional variations, and since we are a much-traveled and basically not a stiff-necked people, many of us enjoy experiencing these differences. However, we like to find, and usually do find, a recognizable framework of social custom in which we can feel at home. It is this hospitality framework with which we need to be familiar.

THE HOSPITALITY FRAMEWORK

Who among us is most in need of familiarity with hospitality customs?

We are all, at times, givers and receivers of hospitality. However, at certain ages and under certain circumstances our need to

know the customs becomes more acute. A few of these age-circum-
stance situations can be suggested here:

1. Parents of young children, if soundly informed in hospitality
customs themselves, can pass their habits on most painlessly.

2. Young couples establishing themselves as new units in a community find this process easier and pleasanter if they can entertain
and accept entertainment with social self-assurance.

3. Families of any age moving into new communities find that
hospitality questions suddenly assume new dimensions. If they are at
home in the basic framework, they will answer the questions without
great difficulty.

4. Unmarried men and women living in their own establishments
—especially young people starting out in life—must build social relationships (give and accept hospitality) or risk great loneliness. This
is always easier with social know-how.

5. People of any age with a strong sociability urge (people differ greatly in their desire or need for social contact) must rely upon
entertaining and being entertained to satisfy it. Their degree of success will be related to how well they play the role of host, hostess, or
guest.

Where do we most often find ourselves confronted with hospitality problems?

The answer is, most frequently, as the host or hostess in our own
home or as a guest in the home of a friend. We cannot conduct *en-
during* and satisfying social relationships on street corners, in the
supermarkets, in club meetings, at church affairs, hotels, summer
resorts, or other places of public gathering. To achieve *depth* in our
human companionship we must know our friends in their homes and
in ours.

Of course, institutional and public meeting situations are valuable for many reasons—not least among them the opportunity they
give the stranger to become acquainted. The socially active person
will also often find himself in a host or guest situation in his club,
church, or school activities. This will not differ essentially from the
hospitality framework of the home. It will be an easy adjustment for
the person who understands hospitality.

What makes for successful hospitality?

This question involves many aspects of social usage that are discussed elsewhere in this book. Specific information about issuing invitations, making introductions, behavior at table, table-setting, and so forth, should be sought in the chapters on these subjects. We are concerned in the present chapter with successful hospitality as it depends upon success in the contribution of host, hostess, guest. Let us look first at what is required of the successful host and hostess.

THE SUCCESSFUL HOST AND HOSTESS WILL . . .

. . . plan ahead. They will list all essentials for their entertainment: flowers, cigarettes, food, etc.

. . . avoid a keeping-up-with-the-Joneses atmosphere. They will remember that entertaining beyond one's means is in very poor taste.

. . . never invite more guests than they can take care of comfortably. To do so is no compliment to the guests, who will be made uncomfortable in this situation.

. . . never ask an invited guest who is a celebrity to sing or perform. If they expect him to entertain their guests, they should make this arrangement with him and pay him his regular fee. If he is a guest, he sould be treated as a guest.

. . . never urge a guest to drink or to have repeated drinks. This may embarrass the guest.

. . . never urge guests to stay if they want to go home.

. . . bring together congenial people who have mutual interests. This obviously lowers the conversational hurdles and is perhaps the most important of all hospitality reminders.

. . . introduce new blood into a group of habitual companions whenever this is possible and suitable. This prevents such a group from going stale, enlarges the circle of friends, and stimulates conversation.

. . . entertain for their own and their guests' satisfaction and happiness, not merely to reciprocate.

. . . pay special attention to the shy guest, the strangers, and the less well-acquainted guests.

. . . ask permission to call or arrange to have a friend call for a single woman and see her home. She may, of course, have her own car and prefer to use it or to make her own arrangements.

. . . make their entertainment conform to the likes and dislikes of the guests, not vice-versa. They will not force sugar-foods on a diabetic, alcohol on a nondrinker, or rich cakes on one who is dieting. They will not insist on a game of bridge if their guest hates cards. They will make a point of remembering the habits, food idiosyncracies, and interests of guests whom they entertain frequently.

. . . make light of accidents. As the poet Lowell said, "Mishaps are like knives, that either serve us or cut us, as we grasp them by the blade or the handle." The thoughtful host and hostess will eliminate the cause of accidents in so far as is possible. If you provide large ash trays and empty them frequently, guests will be happy and the furniture safe.

. . . discourage guests from forming tight little groups at a large party, but will not interrupt or make impossible the holding of interesting conversations. They will themselves circulate and will tactfully urge guests to do the same.

. . . be alert to their guests' needs but will not "fuss" over them. A guest is made uncomfortable by being constantly asked about his comfort.

. . . not inflict pets or hobbies on guests whose enthusiasm for such things appears cool.

. . . try to keep children (especially their own children) in low visibility at adult parties. They will do this by making special arrangements or providing special entertainment for both their own and guests' children.

. . . see to the door guests who are leaving or if it is night, the host will see a lone woman to her car. He will not leave his other guests to see a couple to their car, however.

. . . always do the best that they can with what they have and without apologies. Ingenuity, congenial companionship, and moderate novelty can often be made to substitute for expensive food, furnishings, and entertainment.

ENTERTAINING HOUSE GUESTS

The successful host and hostess will . . .

. . . in extending their invitation, let their guests know what activities to expect, and will tactfully suggest what type of garments and accessories may be in order (swim-suit, evening dress, golf clubs).

. . . prepare for the comfort of their guests to the best of their resources and ability. The guest room should have . . .

    . . . adequate space for hanging clothing and enough clothes hangers.

    . . . a convenient place for setting and opening a suitcase.

    . . . a good mirror.

    . . . an electric outlet.

    . . . a reading lamp.

    . . . an alarm clock.

    . . . an ash tray.

    . . . a glass for water.

    . . . a box of tissues.

The room may also provide . . .

    . . . a new toothbrush for the forgetful guest.

    . . . writing equipment.

    . . . a sewing kit for emergencies.

    . . . a clothes brush.

    . . . aspirin.

    . . . a few flowers.

. . . tell their guests at what hours meals will be served and when other activities are planned. The guest who prefers sleep to breakfast will be urged to make himself or herself at home—in other words, to go ahead and sleep.

. . . ask their guests how much time they need for dressing before breakfast, and will call them in time. They will *not* call a guest an hour before breakfast when a half-hour is all he has requested. (Of course, the guest may prefer to depend upon the alarm clock, if it has been provided, and thus relieve his hostess of the calling responsibility.)

. . . allow their guests some free time to pursue their own interests and will not interrupt them when they are reading or writing letters, napping, and so on. At the same time they must not neglect the lonely or shy guest who isolates himself out of embarrassment.

. . . not hesitate to suggest that it is bedtime, when the day's activities are over. Guests are often grateful for this, although they may have hesitated to make the suggestion themselves.

THE BACHELOR HOST WILL . . .

. . . never be in the kitchen mixing drinks while his guests are arriving. He never greets his guests with a drink in one hand and a cigarette in the other. This is very rude. He may ask a bachelor friend to act as bartender, empty ash trays, and clear away used glasses.

. . . greet each arriving guest and mingle with his guests, introducing them. He may ask the wife of a friend to act as hostess, although this is not necessary. He never invites an unattached woman to act as hostess, unless they are formally engaged. He may, of course, ask his sister, his mother, or another close relative to serve in this capacity.

THE UNATTACHED WOMAN . . .

. . . will follow the same rules as any hostess, with one exception— at a sit-down dinner, since there is no host, she will need to function as both host and hostess. She may ask one of the male guests to help mix the drinks. She may also, of course, ask a male relative to assist her.

. . . if she is entertaining in a restaurant, she should handle all of the details of the party before it takes place, and particularly she should make all financial arrangements in order to avoid embarrassment to the men who are her guests.

THE POPULAR GUEST WILL . . .

. . . be prompt in accepting or regretting an invitation. Entertaining requires considerable planning and effort on the part of host and hostess. It is inconsiderate to ask them to wait for a reply.

. . . arrive close to the scheduled time and will leave close to the suggested time. An alert guest catches the "party's over" signals and never overstays his welcome.

. . . if he is the guest of honor, arrive ahead of time and remember that no one can leave before he makes the move to go.

. . . if he must leave early, go first to the hostess with his explanation and apology and then go with her to the guest of honor to bid good-bye.

. . . never ask anyone (someone unexpectedly returned to town, perhaps) to go with him to a party without first consulting the hostess. If the occasion is a dinner, and the invited guest is responsible for the unexpected returnee, the invited guest will explain this to the hostess and then will regretfully decline the invitation. If the occasion is a buffet, a tea, or a cocktail party, however, the invited guest may ask permission to bring along his own guest.

. . . always thank the host and hostess before leaving. This should be followed in a day or two by a phone call or note if the occasion has been something special or if the guest has been entertained for any but the most casual meal.

. . . always offer to assist the host or hostess in the necessary details of chair arranging, table preparation, and so on, but will never press the offer to the point of embarrassment. House servants are relatively rare in our time, and the guest who is willing to help is likely to be a frequently invited guest.

. . . observe scrupulously careful smoking manners. He will never use a cup or saucer for an ash tray or flick ashes on the house plants. He will be particularly careful never to let a live ash fall on table linen or rugs.

. . . never lean back on the rear legs of chairs (this dents the floor and may break the chair) and never puts his feet on the upholstered furniture.

. . . have neat bathroom habits. He will never leave a dirty or soapencrusted basin. Dirt should be *washed* from the hands or face, not wiped off on the towels, and towels should be replaced neatly on towel bars. Lipstick should never be wiped off on linen towels.

. . . always pay for any telephone toll calls he makes and will use the telephone very briefly and only when absolutely necessary.

. . . never set wet or hot glasses or dishes on unprotected furniture, or dog-ear books, or otherwise abuse his hosts' possessions.

. . . if he has a cold or is otherwise sick, make last-minute regrets rather than "suffer through" the occasion and probably pass along the cold to everyone present.

. . . if asked, always express a preference (probably a choice of food or entertainment) rather than reply, "Oh, just anything is all right," or "It doesn't matter."

. . . always be polite and amiable to fellow guests, and will do his best to contribute to conversation, games, or any other aspect of the entertainment. He will avoid subjects known to be bitterly controversial, but he will not hesitate to talk about subjects of interest where some difference of opinion may add spice to the conversation.

. . . avoid long good-byes at the door.

. . . make an effort to reciprocate the kindness of his host and hostess in some way. This may take place naturally and in the course of time through a return invitation. Where this is not feasible, the guest may anticipate the problem by bringing a gift with him if the occasion seems to warrant this, or he may send a note of thanks, or a note and gift after the event. The gift should not be ornate or ostentatious. It could be a box of candy, a book, a few flowers, or some novelty for the house. It might also be a toy for the children. A guest frequently entertained in the same home would not attempt to requite each invitation separately. A Christmas, anniversary, birthday, or other special-occasion gift would be quite suitable in this instance.

THE HOUSE GUEST WILL . . .

. . . if the invitation has not been specific as to clothing and accessories, ask his hostess or host about this before packing.

. . . conform to the habits of the family he is visiting and join enthusiastically in the proposed plans.

. . . show an interest in all members of the family—children and older persons as well as those of his own age.

. . . offer to help with the household chores and will cheerfully walk the dog, read a book to the toddler, or wipe the dishes.

. . . keep his own room in order and his possessions out of the way. He will make his own bed unless there is a maid who performs this task.

. . . make plans of his own only *after* consulting his host or hostess. If the guest has other friends in the same community, he may wish to accept invitations from them, and this is quite permissible so long as he does not disrupt plans made for him by his host and hostess.

. . . when he leaves, take his possessions with him and not put his friends to the nuisance of sending forgotten clothing, jewelry, and so on.

. . . if there are servants, be polite and considerate. It is sometimes in order to leave a tip for servants if the guest has caused them to have extra work. (See page 228.)

. . . never be late for meals if he can possibly avoid it.

. . . not make a habit of borrowing equipment or clothing from his host or hostess—golf clubs, swimming trunks, sweaters.

. . . not tag along to parties or events to which he has not specifically been invited.

THE LARGE PARTY

Warm hospitality on a large scale introduces some entertainment situations which can seldom be handled by host and hostess alone. They cannot at one and the same time receive guests at the door, direct them to dressing rooms, introduce them to the guest of honor and other guests, oversee the refreshment service, and circulate through the gathering to assure the mingling of individuals and groups. Some fairly well-standardized procedures are in order for solving this assistance dilemma. Depending upon the number of guests and the physical layout of the rooms, and assuming that professional service, if used at all, is limited to catering, the following hospitality-aides (close friends or relatives of host and hostess) will be needed:

1. One or two door-receptionists who will admit the guests, ask their names if they are unknown, welcome them, and direct them to dressing rooms where they may leave their coats.

2. One or two hall-receptionists who will steer or direct guests leaving the dressing rooms to the main party and will indicate the receiving line or the whereabouts of the hostess. If the party is a mid-summer affair and the guests bypass the dressing rooms, or if the

	five–six o'clock	*six–seven o'clock*
Open door, greet people, tell them where to take wraps.	Jim and Ann Stanley	John and Jane Adams
Pour tea or coffee.	Grace Black	Louise Smith
Assist at table.	Margaret Hall	Ann Gould
Take cups to kitchen when people are finished.	Jane Smith Shirley Brown	Barbara Davis Jean Lester
Floaters, to introduce strangers, and take care of shy guests.	Jim White George and Sally Dodds	John Land Tom and Dianne Douglas

room arrangement is compact, the door-receptionists may double as hall-receptionists.

3. One or two receiving-line aides, if the party is very large, who will be alert for incoming guests and who will pass the guest along to the hostess at the head of the receiving line.

4. A variable number of floaters, depending upon number of guests and degree of strangeness. Several floaters should be stationed

near the end of the receiving line to start the guests mingling with each other. Other floaters should be available to rescue the shy and to introduce strangers.

5. One or two hostess-substitutes, who are designated to pour if the party is a tea. (See Chapter 7.)

6. One or two host-substitutes to tend bar if the affair is a cocktail party. (See Chapter 7.)

7. An adequate number of service-aides, if professional help is not being used, to keep the refreshment tables supplied, used cups and glasses collected, ash trays emptied, and so on.

8. Special host or hostess-substitutes specifically assigned to attend to the comfort, introductions, and occasionally, protection of eminent guests, elderly guests, or others to whom special deference is due. At student-conducted college affairs, a student hospitality-aide should be assigned to each faculty member present.

It is often helpful to make out a schedule for hospitality-aides beforehand. Such a schedule might be as on page 127.

THE RECEIVING LINE

The receiving line is a useful device, through which all guests at a large party may meet the guest or guests of honor. It serves the incidental function of letting the hostess know who is present. Ordinarily, a guest goes down the line as soon as possible after arriving at a party. However, if everyone arrives at or near the same time it is not necessary for guests to wait their turn in military formation. The overflow may mix with the rest of the party, chat with friends, and even accept refreshments while waiting for their chance to be received. They must not neglect the receiving line, however. Going down the line is a *must* of this social situation.

The hostess stands at the head of the receiving line; on her right is the principal guest of honor, followed by others whom the occasion may be honoring. At a college affair, this might include several heads of departments, or visiting professors.

What do you do when you go down the receiving line?

When a man and a woman are together, the woman always precedes the man in going down the line. The woman shakes hands with the first person in line and says, "How do you do? I am Mrs. Brown." She does not mention her first name. The man shakes hands with the first person in line and says, "How do you do? I am Ralph Brown." If Mr. and Mrs. Brown are well-known to the first person in line (usually the hostess), the name mentioning is superfluous. In this case both Mr. and Mrs. Brown say, "How do you do?" as they shake hands; the hostess will bid them welcome; each will respond with "so happy to be here," or something of the sort; the hostess will introduce them to the next person in line; and this person will introduce them to the next person—and so on down the line.

The guests move down the line promptly, keeping their greetings and conversations very brief.

At private entertainments the receiving line is kept as short as possible, sometimes including only the hostess and guest of honor. Practice varies regarding the host's presence in the receiving line, but he is usually included and will be stationed just below the guests of honor. Of course, if the host is himself an important person or the person for whom the party is being held, he is always in the line, either in the position of guest of honor or as close to the head of the line as is practicable.

The receiving line at a large, closely-organized entertainment may be required to stand for a considerable time while all the guests are introduced. Chairs should always be available for guests who are in the receiving line so that they may relax during lulls in the flow, or while some lengthy conversation may be taking place further up the line. Since guests attending at-homes and teas or cocktail parties may arrive and depart over a period of several hours, the members of the receiving line will sit in or near their places during most of this time and will be served refreshments there. They need rise only to receive the scatterings of new guests as they arrive to be introduced.

10

Invitations and Replies

If we are to move successfully and easily in our human relationships, it is not enough that we are able to speak and to write. We must also conform to patterns of the spoken and written word acceptable to our time and culture. Elsewhere in this book we discuss use of the spoken word in our conversational needs and use of the written word in our personal and business correspondence. There is one other social situation in which "manners must adorn knowledge" in our use of language. This is when we issue and reply to invitations. It is no news to any of us that manners have a tendency to jell, and to change with extreme slowness. Social expectation as regards invitations and replies is such a pattern-bound area. We may live long and uneventful lives without ever mastering these patterns, but we may live happier and socially healthier lives if we take the trouble to master good usage here as in our other social relationships—thus smoothing our way through the world.

Everyone likes to receive invitations. An invitation implies a party, a good time, a getting-together, even if with only one other person. There is to be a sociable occasion. The mood is suggested by some verses of the last century:

Miss Annabel McCarty
Was invited to a party,

130

"Your company from four to ten," the invitation said;
And the maiden was delighted
To think she was invited
To sit up till the hour when the big folks went to bed.

This was Miss Annabel's first party, and she found it something of a social catastrophe, because the situation involved was one a child could not control or understand. Nevertheless, she found the invitation altogether delightful, as most people, child or adult, would have found it. Someone likes us well enough to invite us to a party —dinner, dance, tea, picnic. What are we going to do about this invitation? Or perhaps the situation is in reverse. Perhaps we like a number of other people well enough to want to invite them to our party. How do we go about it? Good social usage not only shows us the hurdle but helps us jump over it. There are a number of rules we may follow—some general, some quite specific.

SOME GENERAL RULES CONCERNING INVITATIONS AND REPLIES

1. Make your invitation definite. Always include the day, the date, the time (you may set the hour for both the *beginning* and the *ending* of your party), and the occasion (dinner, weekend, dance).

2. Choose appropriate stationery or cards for your invitations. Depending upon the degree of formality you plan, you may decide to have your invitations handwritten, engraved, or printed, and you will need paper or cards suitable for the chosen form. You may decide to use your name cards for the invitations; or you may use the party invitation cards now widely available at stationery stores. Be sure, however, that your choice is neither too garish nor too cute.

3. Use the correct name forms in making out your invitations. Address a widowed friend as Mrs. John Parker, not as Mrs. Jane Parker. Address a man as Mr. Ralph Good, not as Ralph Good. You may safely follow the forms indicated in the chapter on name cards in this book. (See pages 152 and 155.)

4. Indicate on the invitation if you desire a specific reply. Use the initials *R.S.V.P.* (or *r.s.v.p.—répondez, s'il vous plaît*) or the words *Please reply* at the lower left margin of your invitation, or place your telephone number there and the invited guest will know

you expect an answer. *Caution:* Never use a telephone number on a *formal* invitation.

5. An acknowledgment of an invitation is good form, even if no answer is specifically requested. This is particularly true where the exact number of guests could make a difference, as in dining, bridge, or theater arrangements.

6. Reply to an invitation in the same form as that of the invitation you have received. This is not an ironclad rule in informal situations, but it is a safe rule. An informal invitation written in "I invite you" form will be answered in "I accept your" form. A name-card invitation may be replied to by name card, or if a telephone number is given, you may telephone your reply. Formal invitations will be issued in the third person and must be answered in the third person—"Mrs. Peter Gross invites" and "Mrs. Andrew Wills accepts."

7. In accepting an invitation, repeat the day and hour. This insures accuracy for guest, host, and hostess. If you are regretting the invitation, you need not mention the hour, since time is no longer of importance here.

8. *Reply to an invitation promptly and do not change your mind.* If you send your regrets, your hostess may immediately invite someone in your place. It would embarrass her to have to make a last-minute switch.

9. Never resent the request to fill-in for another guest who has sent regrets. This is a compliment to your understanding and indicates that the host or hostess regards you as a real friend.

10. Never take a guest along to a party without first consulting your hostess. And never ask permission to bring the extra person to affairs where the number of guests is important, such as dinners or bridge parties. If your invitation is to this type of party, you must decline, explaining why. If your hostess then regards it as feasible, she may suggest you bring your friend along. If the invitation is to tea, a cocktail party, a buffet, or a reception, you may properly ask permission to bring the extra person with you.

Informal Invitations and Replies

THE VERBAL INVITATION

This is the most casual and least formal of all invitations. It is on a par with "Drop in and see me some time" and usually calls forth the reply, "Thank you, I would love to," and that ends the matter. If you do issue a specific invitation to a friend you meet on the street, follow it up with a telephone call or a note, repeating details.

It is never good form to accept or decline a written invitation in the course of a casual conversation. Always respond to an invitation in kind.

THE INVITATION BY TELEPHONE

This is the simplest and probably most frequent method of issuing informal invitations, and of replying to them as well. Good telephone manners are especially important here. (See pages 36–43.) Be just as accurate in telephoning an invitation as in writing one. Identify yourself immediately and do not expect your friend to recognize your voice. At once, say, "This is Joan Wells. I am having a few friends for buffet supper on Sunday at six and I hope you and John can come." *Don't* say, "What are you doing Sunday evening?" This is a trap and allows your friends no avenue of escape if they wish one.

If you are on the receiving end of a telephone invitation, never hesitate or seem to weigh the desirability of this party. If at all possible, give an immediate and definite reply, repeating the day and hour if you accept. If you decline, it is courteous to give your reason. Of course, you may quite properly need to consult "John" on his plans for Sunday evening, and in this event you must be very prompt in calling your friend back with your reply.

THE INVITATION BY INFORMAL NOTE

A short friendly note may be used for any social occasion not requiring a formal invitation. It is always suitable for luncheon, tea, bridge, dinner, or for a weekend invitation. Through its wording and manner, your note may convey to your intended guest the degree of informality you contemplate. Thus, to a relatively new acquaintance, you may write with considerable reserve.

Dear Mrs. Richards,
     John and I are having a small dinner on Thursday, the sixth of this month, at eight o'clock, and hope you and Mr. Richards will find it possible to be with us.

Do let us hear that we may expect you.

Very sincerely,
Mary Jones

But to more intimate friends you may write:

Dear Jennifer,
    John and I are hoping that you and Bob will join us for dinner at eight o'clock, Thursday, the sixth of this month. If our plans work out, the Saturday morning golf crowd will all be here.
    Please don't fail us!

Affectionately,
Mary

    Your informal note of invitation may, of course, be longer—a real letter—with the invitation as its reason for being. A weekend invitation often requires some detailed suggestions. It is particularly important here that you state clearly the intended date of arrival, the length of stay, the probable activities, and the type of clothing to bring (for dancing, fishing, golf, theater, or city shopping). Your note should include information as to available transportation—bus, plane, train, taxi. Or if use of a private car is contemplated, you might include a route map with highway numbers, and so on. Inviting a guest for "next weekend" is vague and confusing. Does your invitation mean that the weekend starts Friday night or Saturday? Does it end Sunday night or Monday? Avoid all chance of misunderstanding by being definite. Say, "I hope you can be here for dinner Friday, the tenth of June, at seven o'clock, and that you can stay until the noon train Monday, if possible."

    The reply to the informal note must be prompt and definite, as for any other type of invitation. Address the reply to the hostess, but thank both hostess and host for the invitation. Thus:

Dear Mrs. Jones,
    Bob and I will be delighted to accept the invitation you and Mr. Jones so kindly extended to us for dinner on Thursday, June sixth, at eight o'clock.
    Thank you for your thoughtfulness.

Very sincerely,
Jennifer Richards

If the invitation is for a weekend, include in your reply the time of your arrival and of your departure.

The informal note and reply may be written on good white single- or double-sheet notepaper, with or without an engraved or printed heading. It may also be written on a *fold-over card* intended for this and other note-writing purposes. The fold-over will have your name engraved on the front in the same manner as your name card. The note is handwritten on the inside of the card. (See illustration A.) If you need more space for your notes, you may have your name engraved top-center or top-left, and you may then begin your note on the front of the card.

Since formality depends upon the degree of ceremony, we may say that the fold-over card is a somewhat more formal medium for the issuing of an invitation, and for the reply, than the informal notepaper form, but it is never used for the most formal occasions (and it is never used as a substitute for the name card). When a considerable number of people are to be invited to the occasion, the invitation is sometimes printed or engraved on the inside of the fold-over.

THE INVITATION BY NAME CARD

Your name card may be used for almost any informal invitation not requiring lengthy explanation. It is usually too restricted in space for weekend invitations but is more appropriate and convenient for teas, buffets, bridge, cocktails, showers.

Your reply to a name-card invitation may be telephoned, written on notepaper, or replied to in kind, using your own name card. Typical name-card invitations and replies are illustrated here in B, C, and D.

Illustration C shows a name card for a silver wedding anniversary celebration.

Remember that you must not send these cards through the mails in their own small envelopes alone. They must be enclosed in envelopes (of matching stationery, we hope) at least 2¾ inches by 4 inches in size, to conform with postal regulations.

FORMAL INVITATIONS AND REPLIES

As was suggested above, formality is a matter of degree. Almost every type of entertaining may be either extremely informal or ex-

Mr. and Mrs. Robert John Green

WRITTEN PART OF THE INVITATION IS
ON THE INSIDE OF THE FOLD

Saturday, June 6th
Cocktails 5-7

R. S. V. P.
706 Sunset Drive

A. A FOLD-OVER INVITATION

136

Mr. and Mrs. Robert John Green

Saturday, May 5th
Cocktails 5-7

To meet
Mrs. Robert Adams

Mrs. Frank Wilson Cross

Tuesday, April 4
Tea 4-6

B. NAME-CARD INVITATIONS

1920 — 1945

Mr. and Mrs. Robert John Green

Tuesday, June 1
4–7 p.m.

c. A Name-card Invitation to an
Anniversary Celebration

Mrs. Robert John Green

Sincere regrets

May 1

Mr. John Russell Knight

Delighted to come
Tuesday 4–6

d. Name-card Replies

tremely formal in its planning and execution. The nature of the ceremony will accord with long-accepted custom, and the social gestures of hostess, host, and guests will respond to each other as the movements of a dance. The hostess must decide upon the amount of ceremony she desires, and social custom will then carry her along a set course like an automatic pilot. The form of the invitation she issues is the medium through which she lets her guests know the moves that are expected of them. The informal invitations we have been discussing carry one message; the formal invitations we are about to discuss carry another message. They signal Ceremony with a capital C, and in all its splendor. Guests receiving these invitations reply in kind and, if necessary, brush-up their formal-wear wardrobes and their formal manners.

Very definite rules govern formal invitations:

1. They are always engraved or handwritten on high-quality white or off-white notepaper or cards.

2. Headings are never used, but monograms, coats-of-arms, or estate symbols (such as twin pines) may be embossed *in white, never in color*, at the top-center or top-left. For wedding invitations only a coat-of-arms is suitable.

3. They are always engraved or handwritten *in black ink*.

4. They are always written *in third person* and set in block form. (See illustrations below.)

5. Initials *are avoided* whenever possible.

6. Punctuation is used *only* where it is *absolutely necessary*, as in the titles Mr., Mrs., Dr.

7. Telephone numbers are *never* used.

8. Information is conveyed *line by line* in a set pattern (see illustrations below) and never in across-the-page running style as in the informal note.

The reply to the formal invitation follows the style of the invitation. It is always written in black ink on white notepaper and is centered on the first page. It is always written in the third person in block form, one item of information per line. If the invitation has been issued by both host and hostess, you include both in your acceptance or regrets. In regretting a formal invitation (or any other invitation), you need not repeat the expected hour. It is always polite to state your reason for declining an invitation.

The line by line organization of a formal invitation would be:

Mr. and Mrs. George Downing
request the pleasure of
Mr. and Mrs. John Howell's
company at dinner
on Monday, the first of June
at seven o'clock

Replies would be handwritten but similar to the engraved invitations in spacing. Any of the following would be suitable replies to this invitation:

Mr. and Mrs. John Howell
accept with pleasure
Mr. and Mrs. Downing's
kind invitation for dinner
on Monday, the first of June
at seven o'clock

Mr. and Mrs. John Howell
regret that they are unable to accept
Mr. and Mrs. Downing's
kind invitation for dinner
on Monday, the first of June

Mr. and Mrs. John Howell
regret that they are unable to accept
due to a previous engagement
Mr. and Mrs. Downing's
kind invitation for dinner
on Monday, the first of June

Mr. and Mrs. John Howell
regret that because of a previous engagement
they will be unable to accept
Mr. and Mrs. Downing's
kind invitation for dinner
on Monday, the first of June

If you or your children are planning a formal wedding-anniversary celebration, the following are suitable forms for the invitations:

1920–1945
Mr. and Mrs. John Seward
request the pleasure of
(name written in)
company on Saturday evening, the first of May
at eight o'clock
The Pleasant View Hotel

R.S.V.P.
16 Hillcrest Avenue

Jane and John Harris
hope you will come
on Saturday, March first
at nine o'clock
to help celebrate
their parents' Silver Wedding Anniversary

requests the pleasure of

company

on

at   o'clock

E. AN OUTLINE TYPE INVITATION

If you move in a social environment where considerable formal
entertaining is done, you may prefer to use an outline type of invitation. (See illustration E.)

Miss Margaret Addison
accepts with pleasure
the kind invitation of
Mrs. Benton
Mrs. Carlson
Mrs. Curry
for Thursday, the first of June
at one o'clock

Should you receive an invitation from two or more friends who are planning a joint affair (see page 142), you must mention all their names in making your reply. Sometimes, however, such invitations designate one individual to whom replies are to be addressed.

Sometimes an organization—a fraternity or sorority, for instance —issues a formal invitation. This may be phrased as follows, and your reply should be sent to Mr. John Jones, as indicated.

Beta Tau
of
Omega Tau Sigma
requests the pleasure of
your company at a dinner dance
on Friday, the third of January
at seven o'clock
High View Country Club

Please reply to
John Jones
Omega Tau Sigma

It is undoubtedly true that occasions for the use of the formal invitation are not so frequent as in the past. The informal social gathering, at all age and status levels, is now the customary thing— with one very important exception—the wedding. The wedding retains its ceremonialism and glamor almost undiminished. It has staked out a field all its own in the world of etiquette, and the invitation to it, or announcement of it, remain an unbreached bulwark of formalism.

THE WEDDING INVITATION

Everything about wedding invitations, which should be sent out three to four weeks before the ceremony, is rigidly prescribed by tradition and should conform strictly to pattern. The third-person wording of both invitation and reply has remained unchanged through many years. The once ironclad rule that it must be engraved, however, is slowly changing. Engraving is still preferable, but there are processes available now that closely resemble engraving, and are much less expensive. Engraved invitations are undoubtedly the more beautiful, but sometimes it is not worth unbalancing your budget for this touch of perfection.

The wedding invitation (see illustration F) appears on the front page of a double sheet of fine quality white, ivory, or ecru paper. Black ink is always used and there is no adornment, marginal or otherwise. The paper should be large enough to require a once-over fold for fitting it into its envelope, or it should be just right for fitting into the envelope without folding. Script lettering is perhaps the most usual, but there are other suitable typefaces. Be careful to avoid the bizarre and usually unreadable designs.

In your invitations you will find a white tissue, which the supplier has placed there in order to keep the engraving from smudging the white paper. In a damp climate this smudging is particularly likely to happen. You may follow your own desire about keeping or discarding this tissue—there are schools of thought in social usage to support both viewpoints.

If your invitation is of a size to be inserted into the envelope without folding, have the engraved surface facing you as you do the inserting. If it is of folding size, the engraved surface is folded in and the invitation is inserted into the envelope with the folded edge down. The inner envelope is placed in the outer envelope so that the inner one faces the flap of the outer one—what we might call a reverse formation.

The envelopes are addressed in black ink, using abbreviations *only* when they are inherent in the name of the invited guest—Mr., Mrs., Dr. The names of cities and states are always written out. The phrase "and family" is frowned upon. Either send separate invitations to adult children, or if the children are young, include their first names under the parents' names on the inner envelope. Return addresses on envelopes, once frowned upon, may be used when the circumstances make this desirable.

Dr. and Mrs. Thomas Allen Greene

request the honour of your presence

at the marriage of their daughter

Joan Hamilton

to

Mr. William Howard Barnes, Jr.

Saturday, the twenty-seventh of October

at four o'clock

Saint Bartholomew's Church

New York

F. A WEDDING INVITATION

The outside envelope should be addressed in this way:

Mr. and Mrs. John Henderson
65 West Duke Street
York
Pennsylvania   17405

On the inside envelope, you may write either
Mr. and Mrs. Henderson (*no first name*)
or
Mr. and Mrs. Henderson
Joan and Tom

The wording and line organization of the invitation will be as in illustration F.

Should the ceremony be planned elsewhere than in church—perhaps in the bride's home—the invitation will be identical with the church invitation except that the home address will be substituted for the church name, thus:

at four o'clock
409 Chestnut Street
Toledo, Ohio

If the time is to be four-thirty instead of four o'clock, it appears "at half after four." If the bride's mother is widowed or divorced, her name is used exactly as it should appear on her name card. (See page 137.) If the bride's mother has remarried and there is a step-father relationship, the invitation begins:

Mr. and Mrs. Robert Woolworth
request the honour of your presence
at the marriage of her daughter
Mary Ann Thomas

If the bride's parents are not living, the nearest relative sends the invitation, stating the relationship as "his sister," "his granddaughter," "her niece," in place of "their daughter." If the bride has no available relative and the wedding is given by a friend, the title "Miss" is used in front of her name on the invitation.

If the bride is divorced, invitations are not sent to the second wedding. Announcements may be sent, however.

If the bride is a widow, her widowed name is used, not her original given name. She will be "Jane Brooks Hall"—not "Mary Jane Hall."

If the guest list is to be limited to a few friends and relatives, engraved invitations may seem pretentious and the bride may send out informal notes handwritten by herself. Or the mother of the bride may send out written notes.

Military titles are used on wedding invitations only if the groom is on active duty. If the groom is below the rank of Captain in the Army, or Lieutenant in the Navy, he appears on the wedding invitation as

John Allen Fields
Ensign, United States Navy

If the groom is a captain or higher ranking officer in the Army, or a Lieutenant or higher ranking officer in the Navy, the rank precedes his name. The branch of service is placed below the name.

Captain John Henry Worth
United States Army

RECEPTION CARDS

The reception card should be of the same quality and style as the invitation it accompanies. An address for the reply must appear on this card for the convenience of the groom's friends and relatives, who may not be personally acquainted with the bride's family. (See illustrations G and H.)

Reception cards are slipped into the inner envelope along with the invitation to church weddings. They are limited to the guests whom the families of the bride and groom wish particularly to have present at the wedding celebration. They are not included in invitations to home weddings, since an invitation to the home is considered always to include the wedding celebration as well as the ceremony.

ANSWERING THE WEDDING INVITATION

An invitation to a church wedding, by itself, requires no answer unless it is a handwritten note. All handwritten notes must be answered promptly. If an invitation to the wedding reception or breakfast is included, this must be answered. An invitation to a home wedding always requires an answer.

Like other acceptances or regrets to formal affairs, the reply to a wedding invitation is phrased in the third person, even to a close friend, and it is written on the first sheet of white double-sheet note-paper. It is in black ink, in block form, and follows traditional line order. Replies might be arranged and worded as follows:

Acceptance

Mr. and Mrs. Harold Strong
accept with pleasure
Mr. and Mrs. Davis'
kind invitation for
Saturday, the third of June

Regret

Mr. and Mrs. Spencer Nixon
regret that they are unable to accept
Mr. and Mrs. Hall's
kind invitation for
Saturday, the third of June

Combined Acceptance and Regret

Mrs. John Hall
accepts with pleasure
Mr. and Mrs. Spencer's
kind invitation for
Saturday, the third of June
but regrets that
Mr. Hall
will be absent at that time

WEDDING AND RECEPTION INVITATION IN ONE

If the wedding reception is to be held in the parish house or social rooms of the church, or if it is to be a relatively small church wedding and all of the guests are to be invited to the reception at the bride's home, or perhaps a nearby club, the wedding invitation may

Reception

immediately following the ceremony

The Waldorf-Astoria

R.S.V.P.
1010 Park Avenue

G. A RECEPTION CARD

Mr. and Mrs. Percival Harold Clayton

request the pleasure of your company

Saturday, the sixteenth of October

at half after five o'clock

643 Park Avenue

R.S.V.P.

H. A RECEPTION CARD

include the invitation to the reception. Your wedding invitation will then read in its concluding lines,

and afterwards at the reception
The Church Parlors
R.S.V.P.
620 Hillcrest Avenue

THE WEDDING ANNOUNCEMENT

If the wedding is a very private one and invitations have not been issued, an engraved announcement may be sent out on the day of the wedding. This will follow the same pattern as the invitations.

Mrs. James McCracken
has the honour of announcing
the marriage of her daughter
Esther Elizabeth
to
Mr. Sidney Jones
Saturday, the eighteenth of July
one thousand nine hundred and fifty-seven
Saint George's Chapel
Philadelphia

An announcement requires no acknowledgment or gift, but a note of congratulation may be sent, and a gift is always proper if you choose to send one.

*—An established name is an estate in
tenure, or a throne in possession.*

—EDGAR ALLAN POE

II

Name Cards

As with many other social customs, the origin of the use of
name cards, for whatever pur-
pose, is a still largely unresearched area in history. The information
that we do have tells us that some ancient highly-formalized civiliza-
tions in the Orient employed a visiting-card device in social relationships. We know that in our Western culture, as long ago as the
fifteenth century, German students paying duty calls on professors
who were not at home developed the custom of writing their names
on a slip of paper and leaving this as a sign of their good intentions.
We know that aristocratic society of sixteenth-century Europe (the
same society, incidentally, from which our concept of etiquette
evolves) developed an elaborate card-use code and that their artists
vied with each other in embellishing these cards with scenes and in-
tricate designs. We know that the seventeenth century saw the card
in use in England and that by the end of the eighteenth century it
had become much like the plain, unadorned name card of many uses
that we find in England and America today.

We speak of the name card as a card of many uses, and in the
United States today this is very much the case. It has not always been
so, however. In our socially pretentious cultural background, not so
many years ago, it was literally a *visiting* or *calling* card, and the
conditions of its use were prescribed by the socially elect and were
absolutely rigid. If one moved, or wished to move, in the circles of

high society, one paid certain visits to certain people at certain hours of certain days. One was either admitted for an actual visit or one "left one's card," showing that the social obligation had been fulfilled. In official Washington, the diplomatic services, and in military circles, card-leaving routines are still observed. People moving into these social situations and unfamiliar with the customs—especially young married couples in the military service—will do well to acquaint themselves with the expected moves before they are confronted with the problems. Sources of information in this area are suggested in the appendix of this book. (See also page 23.)

Had the name card remained a visiting card in our society, it would now be of little more than antiquarian interest. Customs change with changing social conditions, and the change which possibly has most effectively outmoded the visiting card is the near-universal availability of the telephone. We now telephone before paying a call, and if our friend will not be at home, we do not undertake the visit. Our call has itself indicated our social interest. Also, only in small segments of our society is maid-butler door service any longer a usual situation. Without door-answering servants, the calling card becomes a simple name card to use on those occasions when, unannounced, we call on friends or neighbors and find them out. It is handy in this situation to have a name card to drop in their mailbox or slip under the door, with perhaps a friendly message penned on it —"So sorry to have missed you." Otherwise, as a visiting device, the name card has lost its utility. It has, however, many other functions in today's social, business, and professional world, and these we will discuss briefly.

First, however, let us take a look at the name card. How do social, business, and professional cards differ? All of these have certain standards of size and style. All are white, but the social card may be an off-white, a cream-white. All generally use black ink, although business cards, where display is important, may use brightly colored inks. Large and ornate lettering should be avoided on social, professional, and executive-level business cards. In ordering your cards, the sales person will show you type samples. Script style, when it is legible, is always good. Shaded Roman is good, and there are numerous English and modern American typefaces that are clear, attractive, and distinctive. New styles are constantly being designed, and if they conform to the dictates of clarity and good taste, they are perfectly acceptable.

The size of the card varies, if necessary, according to the length of the name, but the usual size for a married woman's card is 3 to 3½ inches by 2¼ to 2½ inches. An older, single woman—one perhaps in business or a profession—would also use a card of this size. A young unmarried woman, after the age of sixteen, would use a somewhat smaller card.

Mrs. Theodore Raymond

Miss Nancy Fulton Ware

A man's card, regardless of age or status, is expected to be about 3 to 3¼ inches by 1¼ to 1½ inches. The young man, like the young woman, may usefully have personal cards after about the age of sixteen.

The joint card of a married couple will probably be longer than

either of the personal cards. It may be about 4 to 5 inches in length
and perhaps about 2 inches in width.

Mr. William Howard Barnes, Jr.

Mr. and Mrs. William Howard Barnes, Jr.

Pinewood Manor
Short Hills, New Jersey

Name cards for social and professional use are always engraved,
never printed. Business cards, however, where great numbers are
used, may be printed.

SOCIAL CARDS

A young unmarried woman always includes the title "Miss" on
her card, and never includes an address.

The name on a widow's card is identical with the name she used
on her card while her husband was living. She does not suddenly
change from Mrs. John Henry Hall to Mrs. Mary Hall. Unless she
remarries, she remains Mrs. John Henry Hall.

A divorced woman is likely to adopt the name she finds least painful to use. Traditionally, and according to accepted etiquette, she replaces her former husband's given name with her own maiden surname. Thus Mrs. Henry Brown, who was Miss Jane Spencer, becomes Mrs. Spencer Brown. If she finds the use of the name Brown too painful, tradition says that she may go back to her mother's maiden name for succor. Thus Mrs. Henry Brown, who was Miss Jane Spencer, whose mother was Miss Helen Gray, may become Mrs. Gray Spencer. The important thing to remember is that Mrs. Henry Brown never again becomes Miss anybody, and she will probably find using the name Mrs. Spencer Brown the simplest solution to her problem. Custom frowns on her using the name of Mrs. Jane Brown. Her name card will be identical in every other respect with that of other married women.

Mrs. William Howard Barnes, Jr.

Pinewood Manor
Short Hills, New Jersey

A man's social card, as we mentioned above, differs from a woman's card only in size.

The address very often appears to the lower right in this card. Best usage indicates inclusion of the title "Mr." on a man's card from about college age on. A younger boy omits the title.

A man whose name is exactly the same as his father's name includes "junior" on his name card so long as his father is alive. After his father's death he drops the "junior." Sometimes a man's name is exactly the same as his grandfather's name, and his father's name

differs from both. In this case also, he is "junior" or he may choose
to be "the second." If all three men have the same name and all are
living, the second in line is "junior" and the next in line, "the third."
Mr. John Joseph Hall, Jr., or Mr. John Joseph Hall, junior, is correct.

Mrs. John Joseph Hall, Jr., follows her husband's customary
style in name card and in other uses of her name. Her name card does
not read Mrs. John Joseph Hall, junior, if her husband's card reads
Mr. John Joseph Hall, Jr.

Mr. (or Mrs.) John Joseph Hall II or III may also be Mr. (or
Mrs.) John Joseph Hall, 2nd, or 3rd.

Married couples sometimes find it convenient to have a joint
card, usually in addition to their personal cards.

BUSINESS CARDS

Business cards are never used for social purposes. Initials and abbreviations are permissible here. The title "Mr." is omitted on the
business card. Script lettering is not used. The address is always used,
the telephone number is usually used, and the card nearly always

---

JOHN ROBINSON

REPRESENTING
BALDWIN PAPER COMPANY, INC.
233-245 SPRING STREET
NEW YORK   ALGONQUIN 5-1600

---

has the name and address of the employing company. An executive
may have his own name in the center of the card and his firm name
and position in the space beneath this or in a lower corner. Some

lesser company representative will carry a business card having the company name in the center of the card and his own name, with position, beneath this or in the lower left corner. A new employee in a firm, before having his card made up, might wisely consult his superiors as to the preferred form, unless the company itself supplies the card.

BERLIN & JONES CO., INC.
ENVELOPE MANUFACTURERS
ESTABLISHED 1843

HOWARD P. BYK

601 WEST 26TH STREET
NEW YORK CITY
WATKINS 4-4400

PROFESSIONAL CARDS

In general, name cards to be used by people in the professions follow the accepted styles for social usage. A medical doctor's social name card will read Doctor James Hall, whereas his professional card will read James Hall, M.D. Persons holding doctoral rank in other than medical fields may follow this same custom. (In England this custom is routine, but in the United States it is less often true.)

Women physicians and other professionals find themselves in a fog of confusion when their name-card style must be determined. A married woman doctor's social card reads most often, perhaps, simply Mrs. Robert Henry Hill. Her professional card would read Jane Hill, M.D., or Doctor Jane Hill. This is an area of changing custom, and most women finding themselves with professional-title problems can obtain help from their professional friends or organizations.

Name cards to be used by the clergy will probably be the same socially and professionally. The card will read The Reverend William Gould, or Father William Gould, or Rabbi William Gould.

Name cards for use in the military services are particularly important and must be correct. Officers in the regular services must have cards, as must their wives.

Protocol in the Armed Services
and the Diplomatic Corps

Protocol in the Diplomatic Corps and in the Armed Services has undergone changes during recent years because of the tremendous growth in each. The rules have changed and become simplified, but there are still certain procedures to which all officials should adhere.

The term *courtesy* in its military application is assumed to have a double meaning. It implies both consideration for others and respect for authority. It is essential to disciplined living and to effective public service, and the personnel of the various services are expected to behave courteously in all situations.

In the past an official and his wife (either military or civil) were expected to present their respects by making a first call upon all those who outranked them. This has been changed to first calls being made upon a few superiors.

On the initial call the officer or civil official and his wife will make the visit short, not more than fifteen minutes. The impression the wife makes on this call is important, so it is wise for her to observe the few formalities involved. She must not appear nervous. It is she who terminates the call by rising, followed by her husband.

If an orderly (or servant) greets the couple at the door with a card tray, they place their cards on it. Otherwise the tray will be near the door and they will leave their cards there as they enter. In no case are cards left in envelopes. The correct number must be left. The wife leaves one card for each lady in the house who is over eighteen and the man leaves a card for each adult, man or woman. A woman never leaves a card for any male member of the family.

Officers in the Armed Forces are usually briefed on what is expected of them, both officially and socially, when they report to their executive officer upon arrival. Sometimes, however, the commanding officer may prefer to delegate the social briefing to his wife. Probably more often than not, information concerning service etiquette is passed along to newcomers through other officers' wives, and the commanding officer's wife is thought to have this special responsibility.

The rules of protocol are not rigid—each commanding officer of an Army post, Navy yard, or air base decides what procedures he wishes to have followed. Sometimes a special day is set for social calls and sometimes the newly-assigned officers must make their own decision on this. It should be done soon after arrival, however, and Sunday between the hours of four and six is a very suitable time.

Officers are under no official restriction relative to the wording of their cards. This is entirely up to the individual. The wife of an officer places her full name on her card, exactly as does any other married woman. Her address may appear in the lower right corner.

USES OF THE NAME CARD

Socially, the name card has numerous other-than-visiting uses. Two cautions should be noted here before listing some of these uses. First, do not mistake the *fold-over card* for the regular name card. The fold-over is engraved like a name card, but is usually somewhat larger, and while it is very convenient for short notes and informal invitations and replies, it is not a substitute for your name card. It is discussed further in the sections on invitations and letter-writing. A second caution concerns the mailing of name cards. The United States Post Office will no longer accept envelopes of less than 2¾ by 4 inches in size. This means that you must obtain two sizes of envelopes for your cards. The envelopes should be identical in weight and quality of paper. Slip your card into its own little envelope and then into the larger envelope for mailing.

The name card is used as an enclosure with . . .

. . . a gift for any occasion.

. . . flowers for a funeral, graduation, or any other occasion.

. . . commencement announcements or invitations.

. . . any club, public, social announcement, or invitation where the personal touch is important.

. . . Christmas cards. This is very formal and impersonal and is seldom suitable where friendliness is the object.

The name card is used *as* an invitation, and for *replying to* invitations. This is a very acceptable usage for all except very formal affairs, for weekends, or for extended visits. It is discussed further in the section on invitations.

The name card is used as a means of expressing thanks for some small favor, for expressing sympathy or congratulation, or for conveying a brief message to a sick friend who is unable to see visitors—with "hope you are feeling better" penned on it.

The name card is used as a means of letting friends know of a change of address, of letting them know one will be in their city at a certain time, or of letting them know one is leaving town.

Professionally, the name card is sometimes used to announce change of office address, to give office hours or change of office hours, or change of professional status. Some doctors use their name cards as appointment-reminders for their patients, and of course the name card, with handwritten message, is useful to enclose in the "field material" so often exchanged among people in the same or allied professions.

In business, the use of the name card always has economic implications. At the executive level these are restrained and kept within the bounds of social good taste. In the operational and sales areas, economic utility takes precedence and the card is used in almost any way in which it may be expected to further business. It is used in mail enclosures and in personal-contact sales situations. It is a must for business people meeting in conventions or in any other of the numerous business contacts. The business card is never used socially, and the social card is seldom adequate as a substitute for business use.

12

Personal Letters

It was very pleasant to me to get a letter from you the other day. Perhaps I should have found it pleasanter if I had been able to decipher it. I don't think that I mastered anything beyond the date (which I knew) and the signature (which I guessed at). There's a singular and a perpetual charm in a letter of yours; it never grows old, it never loses its novelty. . . . Other letters are read and thrown away and forgotten, but yours are kept forever—unread. One of them will last a reasonable man a lifetime.

—Thomas Bailey Aldrich

The wry humor in this quotation from a letter strikes a familiar chord in most of us. We either have ourselves been guilty of this kind of illegibility or we have often had correspondence with friends who are guilty of it. Possibly the poor readability of much handwriting was a strong incentive for the perfectors of the telephone and of that other eye-saving invention, the typewriter.

The skill of legible handwriting can be learned. The skill—or art —of effective letter-writing, whether by hand or typewriter, can also be learned. Together they add an exceedingly valuable asset to the individual's battery of social and business qualifications and are well worth the expenditure of considerable time and effort in their mastery.

The telephone, as we suggested earlier, has made heavy inroads in the area of letter-writing (and in the use of the name card, as is discussed elsewhere in this book). Telephoning has stepped up the pace of our social and business lives to the point that mailed communications often seem much too slow to be useful. Where utility comes into strong conflict with social form, utility usually wins. We now telephone, or even wire, messages that a former generation would have written by hand according to the precise formula of traditional social usage.

Nevertheless, many social and business situations still require the use of extensive correspondence, and good form, social custom, and esthetic considerations still play a large part in determining the appearance, timing, and content of our letters.

Modern letter-writing has one peculiar problem seldom consciously recognized, perhaps. After our school and college days are ended, and unless our business, professional, or club associations require much correspondence, the ordinary American adult has very little reason to express himself on paper in any respect *except* the personal letter. We become like "Tom Birch," about whom Samuel Johnson reportedly once said, he ". . . is as brisk as a bee in conversation; but no sooner does he take a pen in his hand, than it becomes a torpedo to him, and benumbs all his faculties." Since this "Tom Birch" was in fact a successful writer of his time, we may question Johnson's accuracy or good humor, but we are all familiar with the "benumbed" person who, having or making few occasions to write, finds himself or herself almost unable to do so.

Letter-writing *can* be fun, however. It can even become a hobby, and it can bring much self-satisfaction to the writer and a world of enjoyment to the reader. It can substitute for the rarely-kept diary. In other words, it can be a pleasure if it is approached in this frame of mind.

We have been referring here particularly to the personal letter that one writes to those back home or to distant friends. People on extended vacation or business trips, people who have moved away, far-separated friends and relatives, men and women in the military and diplomatic services—all must use the letter to keep in touch, and writing it they may make a joy or a chore. There is not a great deal that social form, as such, can do to help them.

The letters we are going to consider in this chapter, however, are those that are still regarded as social or business "must" letters, and they conform to widely accepted patterns.

THE BREAD-AND-BUTTER LETTER

This most often follows a visit of one or more nights in the home of a friend or relative. It should follow close on your return from your visit and should be written to your hostess even though you were invited by another member of the family. A man or girl visiting a college friend would write the note to the friend's mother. The letter should be friendly and informal. It should sound sincere and even enthusiastic, but it should not gush. A wife writing for both herself and her husband uses the plural "we" when she thanks her hostess, but signs only her own name. The personal note is much more appreciated than are the widely-available printed cards for this and other purposes. Your hostess has gone to considerable trouble to entertain you. Be equally thoughtful in your reply. Illustrations of bread-and-butter letters follow.

Monday

Dear Mrs Allan,

I can't begin to tell you how much I enjoyed being with you and your family last weekend. The party you gave was simply wonderful and it was so much fun to meet Jane's friends.

I am looking forward to seeing you and Mr. Allan at our next football game.

Sincerely,
John

Tuesday

Dear Jane,

One of the nicest things that has happened to me lately was to be able to spend last weekend with you and Bob.

Your home, as always, is a true expression of your warm hospitality. There is none I enjoy more.

Remember me to Bob, and again many thanks

Cordially,
Cecile

THE THANK-YOU LETTER

A thank-you letter is indicated whenever you have received a gift, as for birthdays, Christmas, a wedding; or whenever you have

June 16, 1959

Dear Aunt Al,

Bob and I are delighted with the lovely silver bowl you and Uncle George sent us. We plan to use it in our dining room where we can always enjoy it. Thank you so very much. We hope you will both come to see us soon.

Love,
Deis

been the beneficiary of some special courtesy or kindness. Perhaps some friend has kindly given you needed transportation from one town to another; perhaps you are indebted to a friend or relative for assistance at a tea. The possible situations in which this note is courteous are almost without limit. The head of the committee (or other member) should always write thank-you letters to chaperons after a college dance and to a speaker who has talked at a dinner. It is safe to generalize that, should the suitability of a thank-you note occur to you, the occasion is one which will make it desirable. In other words, if you think of writing such a letter, then it is probably highly proper that such a letter should be written. This letter of appreciation should reflect the genuine sincerity of the writer, and it will be most effective if written promptly.

THE LETTER OF SYMPATHY

This is of all letters the most difficult to write. Such a letter need not be long, but it must be prompt. Convey your sincere sympathy, avoiding sentimental details and memories—although friends, neighbors, business or club associates may quite naturally express their genuine personal affection for the personality and character of the deceased. Printed sympathy cards can never replace the personal

> Dear Margaret,
>
> I have just heard of your loss and Bob and I wish to offer our deepest sympathy. If there is anything we can do I hope you will not hesitate to call upon us.
>
> Love,
> Julia
>
> Thursday

note, and in many places they are regarded as in very bad taste. Your expression of condolence may be as brief as the one offered for illustration. A letter of sympathy must be acknowledged, but there is no

Dear Julia;

Thank you so much for your kind expression of sympathy. I do want you to know I appreciate it very much.

Affectionately,

Margaret

Thursday

reason for haste here and the acknowledgment may be exceedingly short, as in the illustration. A printed card of acknowledgment is never used in private life, although the death of a public figure may make some such compromise necessary. Note the examples of a suitable letter of sympathy and an acknowledgment.

THE LETTER OF INTRODUCTION

This is a letter written for the purpose of introducing one friend to another friend and in effect asking that some courtesy be shown the bearer of the letter. Socially, it is no longer a common gesture. The ubiquitous telephone has superseded it. If one's friends are expected to meet in some distant place, the letter of introduction is still likely to be used. In this situation, no obligation to accede to the request is necessarily indicated. If such a letter is to be carried in person by the individual to be introduced, the person responsible for the introduction hands the letter over unsealed (a gesture of trust) and the one who will bear it promptly seals it (a reciprocal gesture of trust).

256 Memorial Lane
Chicago, Illinois 60637
June 25, 1968

Mr. George Worth
62 East Fourth Street
New York, New York 10005

Dear George:

It is a pleasure to introduce to you Mr. John Hart, who has up to the fifteenth of this month been on the staff of Harwell and Co., Chicago, as sales manager. Mr. Hart has been asked to take charge of the New York office.

I have been fortunate in knowing Mr. Hart for many years. He is energetic, full of enthusiasm and leadership, among the best of community citizens.

Any aid you are able to give him in his new location will be personally appreciated.

Sincerely yours,

Harry

Harry Smith

In business the letter of introduction still has utility. The letter should be brief and factual. The writer should state the purpose of the introduction, give the pertinent details, which may concern both business and personality, and should then say that he would appreciate any courtesy shown the bearer of the letter.

THE LETTER OF REFERENCE

Like the letter of introduction, the letter of reference has in
many situations been made unnecessary by the availability of the
telephone. However, it is essentially a very important mode of communication, and everyone should have some knowledge of how to

APPLETON–CENTURY–CROFTS

DIVISION OF MEREDITH PUBLISHING COMPANY
440 Park Avenue South, New York, N. Y. 10016

May 1, 1968

Mr. T. Harry Richard
Oblivion Press
1 Park Row
New York, New York 10001

Dear Mr. Richard:

        Thank you for your letter of April 25th inquiring about
Hugo Gulliver.

        He was employed in our Sales Department during his summer
vacations from college for three years. He seemed of good character, and he did work of superior quality. Although we had
looked forward to offering him full time employment upon his graduation from college, he chose instead to enlist in the U.S. Marine
Corps.

        We should certainly not hesitate to employ him again.

                        Sincerely,

                        Carlton Frederick Coatesworth
                        Carlton Frederick Coatesworth,
                        Personnel Manager

CFC:sk

write it. Colleges require letters of reference from individuals who have known candidates for admission to their institutions. Clubs require letters of reference concerning candidates for membership. Employers require letters of reference before hiring employees for responsible positions. Financial institutions often require letters of reference before granting loans or extending credit. The letter of reference can very materially affect the individual concerning whom it is written, so it should be approached with a feeling of real responsibility.

Young people, perhaps, are most often on the asking and receiving end of this social situation, but they may be not very far along the road to maturity before they are asked to serve as references for their friends. It is well to know how to handle such a letter.

A reference letter from a previous employer might be cast in some such form as the above. Length of time employed, character, capability, nature of employment, and reason for termination of employment must always be given.

The character and background reference expected by colleges, clubs, financial institutions, and some employers is more personal but need not be long or detailed.

If you are asked to write a letter of reference for someone whose character or ability you are not willing to recommend, the proper procedure is to politely decline the request. You do not write a derogatory letter or an evasive letter in such a situation.

THE LETTER OF CONGRATULATION

Congratulations are in order when a friend announces his engagement or marriage, the birth of a baby, graduation from school or college, or the achievement of some higher degree. Close friends may provide gifts for some of these events, but non-gift-givers may wish to express their interest and pleasure. Advancement in one's business or profession, the winning of a prize, some public honor, election to office in a club or a community—any of the big events in life—are fit reason for the sending or receiving of congratulations. Here, as elsewhere, the personal note carries more meaning than the many printed cards devised by busy card industries for this purpose. Notes as brief and simple as those below are quite adequate.

100 Peachtree Street
Atlanta, Georgia 30322
May 14, 1968

Mr. Lewis Pasteur Wiley
13736 Giles Lane
Miami, Florida 32319

Dear Lewis:

    Congratulations on your report on the number of un-
inoculated dogs in Dade County. You have demonstrated
great skill in compiling it.

    Let me take this opportunity to wish you success in
your future undertakings.

                         Sincerely,

                        Christain Bernard Worth

CBW:sk

The Writing Paper

It is possible to say that people have three ways of relating to
each other in the social situation. One is the face-to-face relationship
of the everyday personal contact. One is the relationship by voice
alone, as over the telephone; and one is the relationship through the
written word. When your letter goes out to an individual whom you
are neither going to see nor going to hear, the letter is you in proxy.
Therefore, we say, do not only write your message or news with
care, but choose the medium on which you express it with equal
care. In other words, choose your writing paper with the same
thoughtfulness you apply in selecting a dress, suit, or new tie. It will
reflect your taste and your individuality.

In general, white paper, of either smooth or rough texture, is as
correct for most uses as is the white shirt or blouse, for both men
and women. White paper is a must for formal correspondence. Gray,
tan, and ivory or cream are in good taste for other uses, although
men will seldom, perhaps, use the tan. Trickiness in color, shape, or
decoration is to be avoided. Colorfully and sometimes beautifully or

Dear Carol,
        I just heard your
wonderful news and want
to wish you every happiness.
Both you and Bob have
been very special people to
me. Please congratulate him
for me and convey my
very best wishes.
                        Affectionately,
                        Grace

July 6.

amusingly decorated notepaper for informal use has gained wide
acceptance in recent years and can perhaps no longer be written off
as socially unacceptable. For the young men and women establishing

themselves in a community, however, the basically sound choice of writing paper is still the conservative monochrome mentioned above.

Women preferably choose double-sheet stationery, which folds over once to fit into a squarish moderate-sized envelope, or they may choose a smaller size, which slips into the envelope unfolded. Single-sheet paper is also quite acceptable for women and is preferable if the letter is to be typewritten.

Stationery intended specifically for men is always single sheet and is usually longer than a woman's letter-paper and of a size to take two parallel folds for insertion into the envelope.

Personal stationery may have your monogram on it, a family crest (for men only), or some symbol of the name you have given your home—such as "twin pines" or "the crow's nest." Like the monogram, the symbol or crest may appear in the upper-left corner, but more often these are placed at top center of the sheet. A crest of a college club or fraternity is in good taste; a family crest—not often used in the United States—is used only by male members of the family.

It is a common, useful, and quite acceptable custom to have your name, or name and address, printed or engraved on the top center of your stationary (never on formal invitations, however). Customary headings are illustrated on pages 173–174.

SIMPLE AIDS IN LETTER WRITING

Sequence of pages. If a letter is to be from one to three pages long, go from page one to page three and back to page two. For longer letters, the most logical order is the order in sequence—first, second, third, and fourth pages.

Handwritten or typed? Typing of personal letters has not only achieved social respectability, but has become the preferred form of communication if handwriting has any tendency toward illegibility. Use single-sheet paper, space your typing evenly, and type any letter except the following varieties, which good form still requires to be executed in your personal handwriting: invitations and replies, thank-you letters, bread-and-butter letters, letters of sympathy, and the

usual letter of congratulations. Personal business letters of congratulations are typed.

The heading. Name, address, and telephone number may appear in
the heading for all members of a family. It is also possible to use a
family paper with a heading of address and telephone number but
no name, or the family surname might appear (not for formal use).

Headings for business letters must include the firm name and address in full and may appear at the center-top of the sheet or on the
top right-hand side. The name of the state is not abbreviated, and
punctuation is used only for clarity.

Zip code is an essential part of the address and should always be
used for both social and business letters. Place it immediately following the name of the state, as in the business letter example on page
169. Lists of zip code numbers are widely available in many reference books, such as the World Almanac. The numbers can always be
obtained by telephoning your local post office.

Telephone numbers on letter headings may use exchange names
or may be indicated by use of numerals only. People who talk frequently to distant locations can usefully include the area code as a
part of their number. This may be placed in parentheses before the
local number. See the business letter heading on page 174.

Heading styles are illustrated here:

FOR A SINGLE WOMAN

Joan Anne Gates
(*or* Miss Joan Anne Gates)
16 Wellington Avenue
Main City, Oklahoma

FOR A MARRIED WOMAN

Mrs. Lester Arthur Wade
180 Sunset Drive
Plymouth, Maine
(Telephone PLymouth 1-0000)

FOR ANY MAN

Wade Wellington
60 Atlantic Avenue
Ourtown, Ohio
(Telephone WEsley 9-9999)

FOR A BUSINESS FIRM

A. B. Carr Brothers, Inc.
3119 Broad Avenue
Colesville, Kansas
(Telephone CO 8-9000)

The date. If the heading is centered on top of the sheet, the date
may be centered beneath it or, with an eye to spacing, off toward the
right-hand margin; or, in social correspondence, the date may come at
the conclusion to the letter and be entered close to the left margin

on a level with or below the signature. Neither the month nor the name of the day, if used, should be abbreviated. The year is unnecessary in social letter-writing but is, of course, always included in a business letter.

The salutation. The salutation appears at the left margin of your letter. For business purposes it includes the full name and address of the person to whom you are writing, in addition to your greeting. In a social letter, a simple "Dear Sally," or "Dear Mrs. Friend," is sufficient. The following forms are typical:

THE SOCIAL LETTER

Edward Jones
15 Pitts Lane
Hometown, Colorado

June 6

Dear Uncle George,

THE BUSINESS LETTER

1677 Seventh Street
Lincoln, Ohio   45000
June 6, 1959
Telephone (101) 377-7777

Mr. John Page
940 Fifth Avenue
New York, New York   10006
Dear Mr. Page:

Business letters written to firms where no personal name is known to the writer will begin, "Dear Sir," "Dear Madam," or "Gentlemen." These, of course, would be followed by a colon.

The closing. Only the first word of the closing phrase is capitalized, and a comma is used at the end of the phrase. Flowery farewells and stilted endings should be avoided.

The usual endings to a social note are "Sincerely," "Sincerely yours," "Affectionately," "Cordially," "With love," "Lovingly," "Devotedly," depending upon how intimately you know your correspondent. "Hastily," or "Hastily yours," is neither good form nor very complimentary.

The business letter closes with "Yours truly," "Very truly yours," "Sincerely," "Sincerely yours," or, very rarely, as from salesman to customer, "Respectfully."

The signature. The name you sign to your letter must be handwritten even when your letter is typed. Except in letters to well-known friends and relatives, one's full name is signed. However, one never signs a letter using "Miss," "Mrs.," or "Mr." If the title is necessary in order to make one's status clear, it is used in parentheses.

A single woman's signature is "Jane King," or "(Miss) Jane King."

A married woman's signature is "Mary Jane Driver," or she may double-sign her name, first using the "Mary Jane Driver" and immediately under it writing "(Mrs. John Driver)."

A widow signs her name just as she did before her husband's death.

A divorced woman signs her name "Joanne Brown Driver," or "(Mrs.) Joanne Brown Driver."

A man always signs his full name but uses the title "Mr." only if his first name might be mistaken for a feminine name—Cecil, Marion, Francis. He would sign his name "(Mr.) Cecil Jones" in this case.

Holders of high academic degrees, doctors, men and women in high public office, do not use their titles in signing purely social letters. In business, or professionally, they may sign "Peter Abbott, M.D." or "Julius Abbott, Ch.E." or "Roger Forthright, Mayor of Ourtown."

The address on the envelope. The address on the envelope should always include the title "Mrs." or "Miss," unless these are superseded by some professional title such as "Dr." Follow the same social usage as has been presented in the sections *The headings*, *The salutations*, and *The closing*. Use abbreviations only where considerations of space demand it. Always see that your return address is printed, stamped, or written on the upper left-hand corner of the face of your envelope. Mail regulations require this for first-class mail, and personal letters must travel first-class.

You better live your best and act your best and think your best to-day; for today is the sure preparation for tomorrow and all the other tomorrows that follow.

—HARRIET MARTINEAU

13

Dating—
Engagements—
Weddings

DATING

It sometimes comes as a surprise to Americans to learn that dating, as a social custom, is largely a North American invention. Other societies have tended to look upon man-woman relationships before marriage as always being associated to some extent with marriage—that is, if a young man asked to call on a girl, he was at least exploring the possibility of marriage. In our American culture, however, we have learned that young men and young women, boys and girls, can enjoy and profit from each other's company without necessarily being in the least serious in long-range intentions. Dating is our name for this relationship, and dating is now becoming a commonplace in many other countries.

The conventions of dating are not static. In fact, it is possible that they have changed more than any other convention in our society. Nor are dating conventions the same in all parts of our country. They differ widely from community to community. However, there are some basic standards and minimum requirements, and it is these we intend to discuss in this chapter.

176

Social standards and taboos sometimes seem to young adults and to adolescents to exist for the sole purpose of limiting the pleasure of their social lives. Young people should remember, however, that the traditions that bind them are not the invention of their parents and teachers. They have deep social roots, and disregarding custom may have consequences far more extreme than seems justified by some seemingly trivial lapse. A young woman's—and a young man's—good name and social and moral reputation, in our day as in every other period in history, is an asset to be protected. Abiding by the established standards of behavior and manners helps to keep one from being conspicuous and misunderstood. Public behavior should be decent, friendly, and quiet. Personal relationships are most rewarding when conducted with dignity and privacy.

CHAPERONS

One of the major changes that has taken place in dating conventions is the relaxed attitude toward chaperonage. Young people now conduct their dates, in most situations, without adult supervision, although when young teen-agers are involved parents often prefer to remain nearby. The primary purpose of chaperonage has always been to protect a young woman's reputation. Time has proven that a girl's best chaperon is herself. If she has pride and character she needs no other chaperon, so far as her own actions are concerned. She must learn to appraise every person she meets. Each girl, each man, each background, presents a different challenge with different answers. Every individual must find the answers for himself or herself.

Although the individual young woman or young man may be perfectly willing and able to answer for his or her own conduct, society still insists upon adult overseeing—chaperonage—under certain circumstances. Young people of poise and self-confidence rarely object to chaperons at these times. Only the very young and those who are not sure of their popularity ridicule chaperonage customs where they are still enforced.

Mixed parties where all participants are young and unmarried should have the help and security that is furnished by parents or other chaperons. The parents need not be conspicuous and should not try to run the party, but they should be there. This applies particularly to high-school age parties. Parents can see that no alcoholic beverages are served to this age group, that the party ends at a reasonable hour, and that gate-crashers are not troublesome. Parents should not fail to greet the guests and show an interest in them.

Overnight trips, football weekends, fraternity weekends, and so on are other social situations at which society still expects chaperons to be present. Often, in college-age or young-adult groups, some of the group are married and usually are quite acceptable as chaperons.

Chaperons—whether parents or other adults—sometimes have a rather bleak time in performing their duties. The group inviting them should remember that chaperons are guests, and they should be shown every courtesy due a guest. Transportation should be provided for them, and especially for a single woman. Their entertainment should be provided for, and they should not be left alone during supper refreshments or at other times. Members of the group that is entertaining should introduce themselves and their partners to the chaperons and should remember to thank the chaperons for coming when they bid them goodnight. After the party is over, a note of appreciation should be sent to the chaperons.

AT A DANCE

Be a good dancer. This can be good insurance against being left out of party plans. The following suggestions can also help.

The corsage. The young man should ask the girl what color her dress will be before ordering the corsage. This will save embarrassment all around, as the girl will feel that she must wear the corsage, regardless of color and even if it clashes with her dress. If the young man wishes to surprise the girl, he should ask her mother, her sister, or her roommate.

Parking the car. The young man drives up to the door of the building where the party is being held, helps the girl out of the car unless there is a doorman for this purpose, and then drives to the parking area and parks his car. Before leaving the girl, the young man arranges to meet her inside after she has disposed of her wraps. Sometimes the girl prefers to stay in the car until it is parked and then the couple enter the building together.

The receiving line. The couple goes immediately to the receiving line. The girl goes first, introduces herself, then turns to her date as she introduces him. If there is no line, they greet the host and hostess and chaperons. The girl should take the initiative in making introductions if she knows guests whom the young man does not know. The young man should take this initiative, of course, if the reverse is true.

How to ask for a dance. The man says, "May I have this dance?" *not* "Do you have this dance taken?" If the guest of honor is a girl, each man is expected to dance with her. If the dance is a cutting-in affair (a "mixer"), the stag goes up to a girl on the dance floor, puts a hand on her partner's shoulder, and quietly says, "May I?" The man who has been cut-in on thanks the girl and joins the stag line. He must do this with a smile. Couples objecting to sharing dances with others should not attend mixer dances. The man who has been displaced in the dance is expected not to dance with the same girl again until he has danced with at least one other girl.

How to accept a dance. The girl accepts simply by saying, "Yes, I'd love to," "Certainly," or she merely nods and smiles as she gets up to dance.

How to refuse a dance. A girl should never refuse one man and then turn around and accept another. If she really means to refuse to dance, however, she may say, "Thank you, I don't care to dance now." A girl who is dancing is rude if she refuses to change partners when another man cuts in. When a party is announced as a mixer a girl is expected to accept cuts, although she doesn't have to continue dancing with the new partner very long if she does not wish to do so.

The end of the dance. The man always says, "Thank you" to the girl when the dance is ended, or he may say something more enthusiastic. The girl answers, "I enjoyed it," or "It was fun," and she too may show enthusiasm. If a girl wishes to stop dancing before the music stops, it is her privilege to do so. The man is not expected to suggest stopping, however.

Before leaving, after the dancing has ended, the guests must find the host and hostess to say thank you and good-bye.

WHO PAYS?

There used to be an understanding that when a man and a woman were together, the man paid for everything. Today this has changed some, at least in principle, but many men still find it embarrassing to allow the girl to take the check. At all times it is best to be frank about money, but it is boring to dwell on it. Most girls would understand a man's frankness about money, and if they liked him well enough to go out with him at all, they would be glad to accept a date which might include nothing more than the price of a coke.

Among young people, and for business reasons, expenses are sometimes split. This should always be agreed upon in advance, and in order to make it function smoothly, all arrangements should be made in advance in so far as this is possible. For instance, the girl could get the theater tickets ahead of time or the couple could take care of the finances before starting out. Needless to say, young people making arrangements of this sort should know each other very well.

A girl always pays for the tickets for any event to which she has invited a man.

A man does not pay for any expenses during a chance encounter —carfare, lunch check, or phone calls. He can of course do this if he wishes, but it is not expected of him.

Couples who are going out together should always have their arrangements completed in advance to avoid indecision and misunderstanding at the ticket booth or cashier's window.

HOW TO BE POPULAR AND AT EASE

1. The quickest way to make anyone like you is to like him first. Be friendly, smile, and relax when you talk. Let people know you like them.

2. Develop a good personality. Be willing to face your faults and work at changing them. Even physical faults often can be changed—by diet or in other ways your doctor might suggest.

3. Take time to learn the basic rules of etiquette.

4. Learn social poise by being with people whenever possible.

5. Be sure you are well-groomed. A change in style of clothes and hair may be advisable.

6. Avoid affected talk.

7. Tuck away conversation possibilities in your memory. Read in order to talk more easily. Don't monopolize the conversation.

8. Avoid correcting others. Don't be blunt.

9. Cultivate sensitive awareness of the reactions of other people.

10. Don't be over-sensitive or self-centered. Don't carry grudges.

11. Avoid whispering and giggling. Don't nudge, paw, or be a backslapper.

12. Participate in sports and dancing. Others will enjoy being with you.

13. Develop these traits: honesty, cheerfulness, enthusiasm, consideration for parents and their friends.

14. Avoid these traits: conceit, selfishness, and a negative attitude toward accepted customs.

15. Admit your mistakes freely and cheerfully.

16. Be a good sport and see that your blind date has a good time. Blind dates are dangerous unless arranged by someone you know. Men who do their blind dating by telephone are to be avoided.

17. Never, never break a date to accept or seek another. It is inexcusable to stand anyone up.

18. It is never fashionable or in good taste to be late.

19. It is difficult to decide when it is correct to call a friend's date. It would be safer to ask the friend if he or she objected before doing this.

FOR GIRLS ONLY

1. Be ready for your date, appropriately dressed (never keep him waiting more than fifteen minutes).

2. If your date is late, smile and wait for his apology. He may have some very good reason for his lateness.

3. Introduce your date to your parents, house mother, or roommate, as the case may be.

4. Be considerate of the man's pocketbook. Don't pick the most expensive dishes on the menu, unless he encourages you to do so.

5. Don't find fault with the entertainment he has chosen.

6. Be pleasant to your date's friends.

7. Don't primp. Use lipstick or powder your nose briefly, but do go to the powder room to comb your hair.

8. Don't be conspicuous in dress or behavior. Avoid too dra-

matic makeup, chewing gum, and showing off. They will all embarrass your date. Avoid cheapness.

9. If you don't want to smoke or drink, don't. But don't criticize others around you who are smoking or drinking.

10. Don't overlook the little courtesies your date does for you. Thank him for them.

11. Give your date an opportunity to light your cigarette, open the door, help you with your chair in the dining room. Let him help you with your coat and pick up the things you drop. He likes to. If you expect good manners, you will be more likely to get them.

12. Don't, however, expect your date to walk across the room to light your cigarette.

13. Avoid possessive gestures, such as, helping a man with his coat, brushing his clothes, adjusting his tie, or clinging to his arm.

14. Don't keep calling your men-friends on the telephone unless you have some good reason. You may seem to be chasing them, which is still taboo, although the custom of women calling men is now accepted.

15. It is always best to let the man take the initiative in giving presents. Don't embarrass him by giving him a gift if he hasn't planned to give you one.

16. Don't accept an invitation from a man you don't care for just for the sake of having a date or just to be seen with him. This isn't fair.

17. Be responsible toward your date. Don't run to the powder room as an escape. Don't leave your date if you wish to talk to another girl. You should both join the group.

18. A girl should not accept an invitation to visit a man's home unless his mother has confirmed that invitation by telephone or note.

19. If a man doesn't leave when you want him to, say that you have had a good time but had better call it a day. You might mention something you especially enjoyed when you say this.

20. Be a little independent. This gives you an air of confidence.

FOR MEN ONLY

1. A well-mannered young man never boasts about his conquests or criticizes other dates.

2. When you call a girl for a date, identify yourself immediately and be specific by saying, "Would you like to go to a movie Satur-

day night?" Don't trap her by saying, "What are you doing Saturday night?" Make it easy for her to accept or refuse. Never make it a guessing game.

3. When you call a girl for a date, tell her your plans so she will know how to dress.

4. Don't keep asking a girl for a date if she continually refuses you. But if she declines and gives you a reason or asks for a rain check, the chances are she hopes you will call again.

5. Be prompt when you call for your girl, or telephone if you must be late. And don't sit in the car and honk when you call for her. Go to the house and ask for her.

6. Unless you know her very well, you should meet the girl at her home or, if in the city where commuting is difficult, at her office.

7. Talk with the girl's parents before you leave. Discuss with them what time they would like to have her home.

8. When you make a date weeks in advance, it is considerate to telephone the girl a few days before the date. This is reassurance for both of you.

9. It is always the man who thanks the girl for the evening, after he sees her home.

10. Open doors for the girl whenever possible.

11. When on a dinner date, discuss the menu with the girl and make a few suggestions. She has no other way of knowing what you can afford. Usually, you give her order and yours to the waiter. In some places, however, the waiter asks the girl for the order first, then he asks you.

12. After dinner it is up to the man to suggest leaving the restaurant. He knows the plans for the evening.

13. If, at a party, no one is presiding at the punch bowl, serve your partner and yourself. Then walk away from the table so others may be served.

ENGAGEMENTS

Like dating customs, engagement customs differ widely according to local expectations and cultural background. In the United States the formal engagement is considered a serious contract.

As we said earlier in this chapter, dating, in our culture, does not necessarily suggest marriage. Nevertheless, since it is our basic social relationship between men and women, it is the pathway that leads to eventual marriage. Many young people experience what might be called trial engagements before committing themselves publicly to marriage. Teen-agers go steady and symbolize their relationship by wearing identical sweaters, or each other's sweaters, or in some similar way. College students sometimes make quite a ceremony of pinning—and the pinned couple are considered by their friends to be engaged. The formal engagement, however, traditionally involves the couple's parents and a public announcement.

THE TALK WITH FATHER

The parents of the newly-engaged couple should be the first persons told of the engagement. Young people sometimes do not realize that their life plans may greatly influence their parents' future plans—financially and in many other ways. It is considerate and helpful to everyone concerned for the engaged couple to talk over their plans with both families. The man seldom asks the girl's father for permission to wed his daughter nowadays, but it is neither stuffy nor old fashioned to discuss plans with him.

THE ENGAGEMENT RING

A ring is the time-honored symbol of a plighted troth—a formal engagement. It is not an essential element in the engagement, however, and, if used, it does not need to be expensive and should not be ornate. It is wise for the man to consult his fiancée before buying the ring. The man may first visit the jeweler and discuss a possible selection and price range with him. The couple may then visit the store together and the girl make her selection from the rings set before her.

ANNOUNCEMENT OF THE ENGAGEMENT

After the parents of a newly-engaged couple have been informed of the engagement, other members of the family and intimate friends are usually told of it—by telephone calls, personal notes, or perhaps at a family party. Then the public announcement is made.

The announcement may be made at a party held for that purpose, or it may be made in the form of a news release sent to the paper by the girl's family. This is usually done about six months before the wedding is planned, but the time-lapse may be more or less. The date of release should be included with the notice.

To prevent mistakes, the announcement should be sent to the paper in writing—not telephoned. A glossy photograph accompanies the story, which may state, "Mr. and Mrs. Taylor Smith announce the engagement of their daughter Joan to Mr. Robert Craig, Jr., son of Mr. and Mrs. Robert Craig of Detroit, Michigan." This may be followed by a few life-history facts: schools attended by the engaged couple, present employment, and so on. The street address is given only when the people involved live in the city where the paper is published.

If one parent is dead, the living parent makes the announcement, adding, "The late mother was the former Mary Worthington."

If the parents are divorced, the mother usually makes the announcement, adding, "Miss Smith is the daughter also of Mr. John Doe, San Francisco, California."

Announcement of an engagement is rarely made if the woman to be married has been married before. Personal notes are usually sent to relatives and close friends.

Engraved or printed engagement cards, once in common use, are no longer considered good form.

SHOWERS

Showers are most often given by good friends of the engaged couple. Since they are an undisguised request for gifts, they are not given by the immediate families involved. The hostess usually states in her invitation whether the shower is to be general or of a specific kind, such as, a kitchen, linen, or bathroom shower. Traditionally, showers are surprise parties. It is always wise for the persons giving the shower to consult the parents of the bride-to-be on the engaged couple's household needs before deciding on the kind of shower to give.

Although verbal thanks at the time of gift-opening are sufficient in this situation, it is thoughtful for the engaged girl to send thank-you notes. A note should always be sent to the hostess who planned the party.

THE BROKEN ENGAGEMENT

If an engagement is broken before wedding invitations have gone out, no formal notice needs to be taken. If it is broken after invitations have been sent, an engraved or printed card must be sent at once to those who received invitations. This card might read, "Mr. and Mrs. John Doe announce that the marriage of their daughter Joan to Mr. Franklin Smith will not take place."

Wedding gifts already received must be returned with a short note of thanks but no explanation. Shower gifts need not be returned unless the engagement is broken shortly after the shower has taken place.

The engagement ring and other gifts of value which have been exchanged by the couple should be returned.

WEDDINGS

CUSTOMS AND TRADITIONS

Certain customs and traditions have come down through the years to lend dignity to a wedding. People everywhere make a ceremony of marriage. The elaborateness or simplicity of the ceremony is of no real importance, but to ignore the ceremony entirely is usually a mistake. One need not follow every detail of the wedding etiquette too rigidly, perhaps, but a guiding social formula is a great help.

The bride's parents. The family of the bride is responsible for both wedding and reception. Only in rare circumstances are these given by the groom's parents—if the bride is without family connections, for instance, or if her family is abroad.

Invitations. These are laden with tradition. (See Chapter 10.) Send them out three or four weeks before the ceremony.

The groom's parents. Generally, the groom's family makes the first move to call or to entertain the bride's family after the engagement is announced. They also usually offer to give a supper or dinner for the bridal party on the wedding rehearsal evening.

The bridal party. Traditionally, the bride selects her sister to be maid or matron of honor and also includes a sister of the bridegroom as a bridesmaid. The groom selects his brother or his father to be best man and a brother of the bride for one of his ushers. Being asked to serve as a member of the bridal party is considered an honor, and no one should refuse except for some serious reason.

The ceremony. The wedding ceremony differs radically among the various religious faiths and churches. (See Illustrations A, B, C, and D, which show two common forms.) There are available numerous books describing these different ceremonies (see *Suggested Readings*, page 228), and there are numerous wedding consultants and advisory services which will aid in planning the more elaborate weddings. Engaged couples and their families who do not wish this type of assistance can usually find quite adequate guidance through their churches and through the willing suggestions of florists, caterers, and so on. We will make only one point regarding the Christian ceremony here—an often overlooked detail. The bride should go up the aisle on her father's *right* arm so that when the father returns to the left pew to be with her mother he does not have to cross over the bride's train.

Divorced parents. Divorced parents are never seated next to each other in the church. The mother of the bride chooses a member of her family to sit with her in the first pew. Other members of her family sit in the second row. If the father is giving his daughter away, he takes his place in the third row with those of his family he has asked to sit there. If the parents have remarried, the step-father will sit with the bride's mother. The step-mother would be seated in the third row with the father of the bride.

The reception: toasting, dancing, dining. The day of the flowery *toast* is past. Simple toasts are considered in good taste—"to the bride!" "To the bride and groom!" The toast to the bride (the first toast) is always proposed by the groom; the toast to the bride and

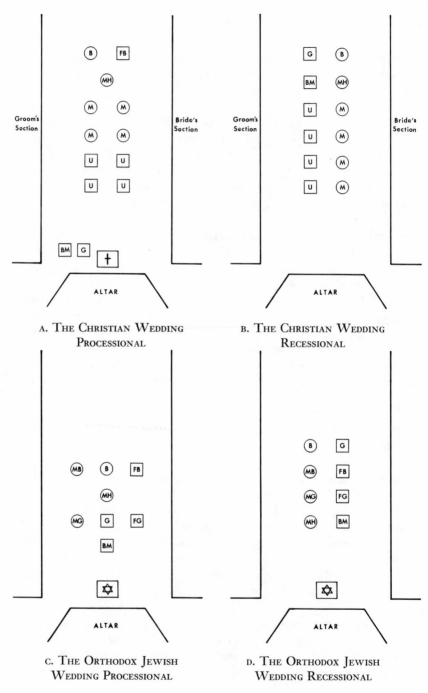

A. THE CHRISTIAN WEDDING
PROCESSIONAL

B. THE CHRISTIAN WEDDING
RECESSIONAL

C. THE ORTHODOX JEWISH
WEDDING PROCESSIONAL

D. THE ORTHODOX JEWISH
WEDDING RECESSIONAL

groom (the second toast) is proposed by the best man. The person proposing the toast should be on his feet, but the person toasted, if seated, never rises and never drinks until everyone else has finished drinking the toast. An appreciative smile is the proper response.

When the *dancing* begins, the bride and groom dance the first dance together for a few minutes. The bride then dances with her father, her father-in-law, the best man, and the ushers—that order.

At the wedding breakfast or supper, the seating follows a very definite pattern. The bride is always seated at the groom's right. The bride's father has the mother of the groom at his right and the clergyman's wife on his left. On the right of the bride's mother is the groom's father and on her left is the clergyman. If there is a separate table for the bridal party, they are seated as in the first example. If there is a combined bridal and parents' table, the seating is as in the second example.

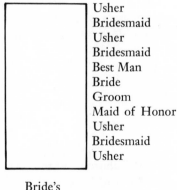

Usher
Bridesmaid
Usher
Bridesmaid
Best Man
Bride
Groom
Maid of Honor
Usher
Bridesmaid
Usher

Bride's
Mother

Groom's Father | Minister
Bridesmaid | Bridesmaid
Usher | Best Man
Bridesmaid | Bride
Usher | Groom
Bridesmaid | Maid of Honor
Usher | Usher
Minister's Wife | Groom's Mother

Bride's
Father

The leave-taking. The thoughtful bride always sends for her parents and the groom's parents to come to her dressing room for goodbyes before dashing off on her honeymoon.

The day after. The newly-married couple should call or send a telegram to both families the day after the wedding to let them know how much they appreciate everything that was done for them.

When the bride is a widow or divorcée. In this situation the wedding should be small and simple. The bride does not wear a veil. If the groom has been married more than once, this need not affect the marriage arrangements. It is the status of the bride that determines the type of wedding.

Over the doorsill. The custom of carrying the bride over the doorsill the first time she enters her new home goes back to ancient Rome. It was thought to be a bad omen for the bride to stumble as she passed through the door, so, to prevent this, the bridegroom carried her through.

FINANCES

The bride's family pays for . . .

. . . the bride's trousseau.

. . . invitations. (See Chapter 10.)

. . . flowers for the church and the reception, the bridesmaids' bouquets, and the bride's bouquet (the groom may ask to pay for this).

. . . church expenses, including aisle canvas, music, sexton.

. . . gifts for the bridesmaids.

. . . the wedding breakfast, supper, reception.

. . . photographs.

. . . transportation for the bridal party to the church and reception.

. . . ring, or other gift, for the bridegroom.

. . . lodging expenses for out-of-town relatives.

The bridegroom pays for . . .

. . . the wedding ring.

. . . the bouquet for the bride (her family may pay for this) and her going-away corsage.

. . . corsages for both mothers and boutonnieres for himself, his best man, and the ushers.

. . . a gift to his best man and to each usher as well as their wedding ties and gloves (if worn).

. . . gift to the bride.

. . . the marriage license.

. . . clergyman's expenses, including his fee or honorarium.

. . . the wedding trip.

The maid of honor and the bridesmaids usually pay for their own dresses, although the bride selects the model and color. The bride is expected to be reasonable about the cost of the dress she selects and considerate of her attendants' likes and dislikes in selecting colors.

The best man, ushers, and fathers all pay for their own outfits (except for ties and gloves). Their suits will be in the same style as that of the bridegroom, whether formal or informal. Many men avail themselves of suit rental service in order to avoid buying suits which they may wear only a very few times in their lives.

DUTIES OF THE ATTENDANTS

The maid or matron of honor assists the bride in every way possible. At the altar she is responsible for straightening the train of the wedding gown, holding the bridal bouquet while the ceremony is taking place, and for taking charge of the groom's ring if one is being used.

The bridesmaids are largely ornamental. They should be careful to keep in step during the wedding procession.

The best man calls for the groom and goes to the church with him at least fifteen minutes before the ceremony. He takes charge of the bride's ring and presents it at the proper time. Following the recessional, the best man takes the minister's fee, which has been put in an envelope, to the church office or presents it to the minister privately after the ceremony. The best man also sees that luggage, tickets, and car are in readiness for the wedding trip.

The ushers' duty is to seat the wedding guests. The number needed depends upon the size of the wedding. There should be enough to seat the guests promptly—about one to every forty or fifty guests.

The head usher, often a brother of the bride, supervises the other ushers in the details of seating families and guests at the ceremony.

The ushers should seem unhurried, dignified, friendly, yet efficient. They speak a few gracious words, in a low voice, as they escort guests to their places.

The ushers should be at the church at least an hour before the ceremony. They group themselves at the left of the door inside the church. When a couple arrives at the church, an usher greets them, offers the lady his *right* arm and conducts her to her seat, her escort following. If several ladies appear, he offers his arm to one of them (the oldest, if there is much age difference) and asks the others to follow, unless another usher appears at that time to help him. Or he may ask them to wait until he can come back. Unrecognized guests are asked, "friends of the bride?" or "friends of the groom?" so that they can be correctly seated—the bride's guests to the left and the groom's to the right of the church.

The ushers may seat the guests regardless of family status if the church seating will not be balanced—the wedding may be taking place far from the groom's home, for instance. No person should be conducted to a seat after the entrance of the mother of the bride. Guests who arrive late must quickly seat themselves or stand in the vestibule.

Although the ushers always go up the aisle in pairs in the wedding procession, this is optional at the recessional, at which time they may walk down the aisle with the bridesmaids.

WEDDING GIFTS

How and when to send. Before the wedding, wedding presents are traditionally sent to the bride, whether or not the giver is acquainted with her. The message on the accompanying card usually mentions both bride and groom. A wedding present sent after the wedding is addressed to "Mr. and Mrs. John Newlywed" and is sent to their new address.

There is, of course, no obligation to send a gift, although it is customary to do so if the guest is invited to the reception. Announcements require no gift, although a gift may be sent if the giver desires to do so. Presents are not usually sent for a second marriage, although they may be sent.

One never need feel that a gift must match the opulence of the wedding. Since the bride may wish to exchange duplicate wedding gifts, it is desirable that the gift be delivered by the store whenever possible.

Arranging the presents. A bride enjoys showing her presents. Her friends like to see them. The thoughtful bride will arrange the gifts to best advantage. They should be grouped to discourage comparison and to conceal obvious duplications. Checks may be displayed but not the amount, or if the amount appears, then the name should be concealed.

Although there is no definite rule as to whether the cards that are sent with the gifts should be removed when the gifts are displayed, it does seem in better taste to remove them. This keeps the person who sent a modest gift from any embarrassment.

The bride's thank-you letters. The bride alone must acknowledge all gifts, whether or not she knows the sender personally. She writes this letter of thanks on plain white notepaper on the day the gift arrives, if at all possible. The note may be short but should express warm appreciation with some mention of the present. Avoid stereotyped, stuffy letters. Although she expresses the groom's appreciation along with her own, she signs her name only, using "Sincerely," "Love," "Affectionately," or "Cordially," depending upon how well she knows the person.

When a present is sent by a married couple, the bride writes to the wife and thanks both, or she may begin her letter, "Dear Mr. and Mrs. Ward."

To send a printed card of thanks for wedding presents is an inexcusable rudeness.

THE RECEIVING LINE

The one fixed rule concerning the receiving line is that the mother of the bride is always first in line to greet the guests. The bride's father may stand in line but more often he acts as host, standing near the line to make introductions. The bridegroom's mother and father always receive with the bride's mother if they are from another town, unknown to the bride's friends. The ushers and best man never stand in the line.

Conversation in the receiving line must be happy and cordial but brief in order not to keep those behind waiting longer than necessary. If there is no one to announce the approaching guests, the guests introduce themselves. It is considerate to help the bride's mother, if she is uncertain of a name, by saying, "John Doe." The bride's mother introduces each guest to the person next in line, who in turn makes the introduction to the person further down the line. Each says, while shaking hands, "How do you do?" or remarks something pleasant about the wedding. It is proper to congratulate the groom but never the bride. The bride tries to repeat each guest's name and if she has a good memory may thank the guest for the gift. To all expressions of best wishes and congratulations the bride and groom need only say, "Thank you."

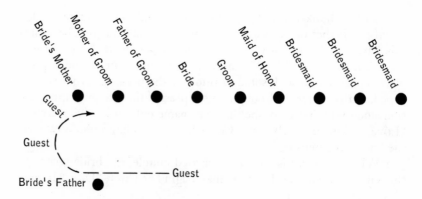

A Plan for a Receiving Line. The Bride's Father May Serve as Host. The Bride's Mother Is Always First in the Line.

Divorced parents do not act as joint host and hostess at the reception. One or the other may give the reception, in which case the parent who is host or hostess would be the first one in the receiving line.

THE WEDDING GUEST

Perhaps of greatest consideration is a prompt reply to a wedding invitation. (See Chapter 10.) Failing to be prompt in this may cause extra expense and trouble to the family of the bride.

What to wear. The choice depends upon the elaborateness of the wedding and the time of day it will be held, as well as upon the character of the community. Women wear afternoon dresses and, of course, hat and gloves for weddings before six o'clock. Men usually wear dark business suits. For an evening wedding the tuxedo is usually worn, although a business suit will often serve. Women wear simple dinner dresses with some covering for the hair—to meet the church requirement. If there is any doubt about what to wear to an evening wedding, a member of the bride's or groom's families should be asked about this.

Guest at the church. The guest should arrive at the church early, and the guest who does so, and is given an aisle seat, is *not* expected to move over and relinquish the seat to a latecomer. The early-arriver merely rises politely and lets the late-arriver pass.

If in a church of unfamiliar ritual, the lead of the other guests should be followed, particularly of the bride's family, unless the ritual calls for something contrary to the guest's faith. It is courteous to conform to the procedure of the church where the ceremony is held.

*We'll have to first make ladies
and gentlemen out of you before
you are of any use.*

—JAPANESE PERSONNEL MANAGER

14

Good Business
Manners

We might rephrase the title of
this chapter "Good Manners Are
Good Business." Whether we
look at the term *business* in the
narrow sense of the bread-win-
ning routines of our lives or in the broad sense of our life work—the
activity which gives meaning and dignity to our efforts—we recognize that good manners will be useful to us and bad manners will be
a hindrance to us. Speaking loosely, business is a way of life and
everyone is concerned with it.

As we have emphasized throughout this book, relationships between people are always more pleasant and productive when courtesy
is practiced. We need not go along with William Cowper in saying
that "manner is all and all, whate'er is writ, the substitute for genius,
sense, and wit," but we can agree that the mannerly businessman or
businesswoman has a better chance of success than his unmannerly
counterpart. In business in the narrow sense—and this is the sense in
which we will use it in this chapter (*business:* "a way of making a
living")—we need to be alert to every factor that will advance us and
on guard against every factor that may hold us back. Good business
manners are like an investment in United States government bonds.
Once they are acquired, they go on quietly increasing in value. They
are the soundest kind of an investment. An easy, courteous, relaxed

196

bearing, tact, friendliness, and social know-how are as good as money in the till.

The basic principles of business manners are the same as those of good manners in any area of life. Only the social situation is different and we must accommodate our responses to this difference.

THE BUSINESS SITUATION

What is the business situation? We may define this situation briefly and narrowly as any human-relations situation in which two people are seeking material profit. They may be working together to seek profit, or they may be on opposite sides—as in the buying-selling situation. The profit may be money, or it may be some other material advantage.

We may become involved in this situation quite early in life, in summer jobs, after-school jobs, even in helping around the home; or we may not meet it in any real sense until we have finished our formal schooling. Most often, perhaps, we meet the business situation and recognize its newness in our experience when we make our first attempt to get a job. To some people jobs seem to come as easily and effortlessly as a summer rain, and with some people they are of equally short duration. Some people find job-hunting so disagreeable and threatening that they panic at every effort and give a very bad impression of themselves. Such people, once fixed in a job, may cling to it with all the desperate need of a small child clinging to its mother rather than face the hazard of unemployment again. One's reaction to job-hunting is an aspect of one's personality adjustment, and the problems that arise may need much deeper help than can be found in a discussion of the mannerly approach to business. However, knowledge of this approach and some awareness of business routines, techniques, and attitudes may lessen the fears and greatly increase the self-confidence of the person of average personality adjustment. Obviously this is desirable and is worth some study.

APPLYING FOR A JOB

When you apply for a job you are selling a valuable and important piece of merchandise: yourself. Present yourself as favorably as possible. You are fortunate if you can make yourself realize that, from the moment of your first job application, your *business record* has begun. Everything you do from this first gesture to the end of your career becomes a part of that record and will help or hinder your progress. Therefore, never apply for a job unless you are prepared to make an honest effort to fulfill its requirements. Later employers will not object to a record of numerous trials and failures if honesty of effort can be shown. It is sometimes only in this way that we can discover our most hopeful abilities or latent skills. Later employers will, however, object to a record of fitful starts, antagonistic deportment, and hasty and frivolous departures. Honesty, reliability, tenacity of purpose, and good manners are the building blocks of the successful person in business.

THE SUMMER JOB

For the college and high-school student and teacher the summer job has become a work area of extreme importance, both from the experience angle and the money-making angle. It is of great importance also as a proving ground for one's ability to get along with other people in the work situation. Your manners, or lack of them, will be highlighted here as they are in your life-work job.

It is in the summer job that the young person has his or her finest chance for acquiring broad work experience. We list here some areas of that experience—all of them close-contact human-relations situations, in which the value of tact and good manners are fairly obvious. People interested in working in these areas can learn more about them by going to their public libraries, consulting local chambers of commerce and employment agencies.

Camp counsellors, playground workers, community recreation program workers

Resort and hotel workers—waiters and waitresses, busboys, kitchen help, beach boys

Gas station attendants

Postal-worker substitutes

Factory-worker substitutes

Railroad workers and substitutes

Business office substitutes

Theater workers

Travel agency workers

Tutoring and summer-school assistants

Store-personnel substitutes

"Outside" sales personnel for magazines, encyclopedias, or other summer sales campaigns

Agricultural workers

Handymen, house painters, building workers

Hospital and institutional social service workers and substitutes

There are, of course, many more possibilities. Everywhere that people work there is the possibility of summer work for students.

How to find the job. If you know the type of job you want and the location in which you wish to work, you should proceed with your job-hunting in exactly the same fashion as you will do when you look for your full-time job.

If you are "playing the field" in the hope of finding something both congenial and remunerative (remembering always that once you are committed you have a responsibility to stay with the situation), you may do any or all of the following things:

1. Go the rounds of all the summer-job possibilities in your neighborhood: gas stations, highway stores, supermarkets, restaurants, etc. Do this in person. Be neat. Be polite. And be prepared for gruff rejections as well as polite brush-offs.

2. Register at your nearest United States Employment Office. If you get a job through this office, you will not have to pay a fee. You may also register at private employment agencies if they handle summer help but make sure the fee in this instance will not take too large a share of your profit.

3. Read the local newspaper want ads and those of nearby cities and towns. Do this immediately after the papers come out. By "this afternoon" or "tomorrow" the job will probably be gone.

4. Place your own ad in these papers. This is usually very inexpensive and the returns are often very good.

5. Let your friends and your family's friends know that you are looking for work.

6. If work is so scarce that you are faced with an idle summer, try to get volunteer work with some social agency or public or private institution (hospitals, homes or camps for underprivileged children, etc.), or build up your private business in baby-sitting, dog-tending, grass-mowing, odd-jobbing, etc.

THE PART-TIME JOB

In the United States the part-time job seems to have become a fixed element in our employment pattern. Students, teachers, and housewives as well as a considerable number of retired persons form the great worker reservoir into which business and industry dip at need.

Like the summer job, the part-time job may be a horizon-stretcher for a young person not yet ready to enter upon full-time work. Or it may be a needed income-stretcher for housewives and retired persons as well as for students and teachers. Like the summer job, it may be found wherever work is being performed, but it is not so likely to have a seasonal character.

The person looking for part-time work should not hesitate to apply to any business concern in which he or she may be interested. Light industry, retail stores, and business offices quite frequently use workers in this category. The person with office skills has little difficulty in finding acceptable work, hours, and pay in this field. The untrained person is perhaps more likely to find opportunity in retail sales or in light industry. The same job-hunting methods apply here as apply for the full-time job or the summer job, and the same personality and social adjustment traits will be of value here as are of value in these other categories.

THE FULL-TIME JOB

Upon graduating from college or high school, you may acquire your first full-time job in any of several ways: the placement service of your school may put you in contact with your job opportunity; you may be in a worker-shortage field, such as engineering, in which case the job is likely to find you before you have graduated; or you may have to get out and scramble for your job in much the same way as you have gone about getting summer jobs. In any event, your job-hunting effort may require the writing of a letter of application and it will certainly require an interview.

THE LETTER OF APPLICATION

This should be typed on a single sheet of paper with a heading and a complete date. It should be as complete and as brief as possible. Your letter will be given prompt attention if you are able to obtain the correct name and title of the person to whom the letter of application should be addressed. A model for a letter of application is illustrated below: [1]

Street or Dorm Address
City and State
Date

Name of person to whom the letter is written
His title
Name and address of the business
City and State

Dear Mr. ———:
    (Paragraph 1) Begin your letter by stating how you learned of the position. Outline your understanding of any unusual requirements of the position.
    (Paragraph 2, or Paragraphs 2 and 3) Show how your experience and education fit the requirements for the position open or the type of work for which you are applying.
    State facts in such a way that the recipient will think well of you and feel that he would do well to see you and go further into the subjects on which you touched in your letter.
    You may include your references here, but you must be sure you have permission from your references to use their names.
    The employer knows you want a job with adequate pay. Therefore, do not feature this subject even though it is of tremendous interest to

[1] *From* a Sample Letter of Application, used by the Teachers Placement Division, The Pennsylvania State University.

you. Make him feel that he would profit by your services, now and in the future.

(Paragraph 3 or 4) As the primary purpose of a letter of application is to secure an interview, ask for it in this paragraph. If you plan to be in the vicinity sometime in the future, you might suggest dates when you could be available, such as during the Christmas Vacation. Otherwise, let it be at the administrator's convenience.

Sincerely yours,

(Sign your name)
Type your name

THE INTERVIEW

Industry and business spend thousands of dollars every year interviewing people. Your college or high-school scholastic record they can obtain inexpensively through the mail. Your references can be consulted with relative ease by mail, telephone calls, or even by personal visiting. The company wants more, however. It wants to see and talk with you. It wants to weigh your character and behavior as they appear under the stress of an interview.

To prepare yourself for the interview, study the following checklist:

1. Find out everything you can about the firm before going for the interview. You can then ask intelligent questions and can talk about yourself in terms of the needs of the employer.

2. Be prompt! You start with several strikes against you if you come one minute or ten minutes late. Excuses are seldom of value in this situation.

3. Try to make a good first impression. Your interviewer will see you before he hears you. Be well-groomed, neatly and appropriately dressed. Be sure your hair, nails, gloves, and handkerchief are neat and clean. Avoid strong perfume, college jewelry, and conspicuous clothes. (See page 204.)

4. Be alert and responsive. Avoid the frozen apathetic look. Your facial expressions, body mannerisms, and voice quality, as well as what you say and your speech traits, are character indices. Your interviewer will be looking for emotional stability and individuality. Don't fidget.

5. Let the interviewer offer his hand first. This is good advice

for women as well as for men, in this situation. Say, "How do you do?"—*not* "Hello."

6. Don't smoke, unless the interviewer is smoking and offers you a cigarette. Particularly, never walk into a job interview smoking! and never walk into a job interview chewing gum!

7. Wait to be invited to sit down before you take a chair.

8. Look at the interviewer when you speak to him (without staring, of course). Keep your voice low. Avoid nervous gestures.

9. Don't rush the interview. Let the interviewer ask questions and set the pace. If the interviewer seems to be in a hurry, present your story and get yourself out as quickly as possible.

10. Answer questions honestly and politely. Omit irrelevant material. Briefly describe whatever you feel has fitted you for the job. Don't pretend to know everything. No one expects that.

11. If this is not your first full-time job, you will be asked to explain why you left your last job. Avoid criticism of your recent job or employer. This is most important. Under no circumstances carry tales from one employer to another. Say, "I wanted to get into a different field," or "I wanted a change of location," or "I felt that I was at a dead end, and I wanted a job with a future."

12. Let the interviewer bring up the salary question. This is a ticklish question. If possible, get the employer to make an offer. If you make the first suggestion, you may have to settle for less than the employer was prepared to pay, or you may ask for so much that you forfeit your chance for the job. In many types of work it is possible to learn from the ads, from friends, or from job statistics, which may be found in libraries, just about what the customary salary is for a person of your qualifications. Don't bring the subject up, however, unless the interview is about to close with a good chance of your being hired without knowing the pay.

13. Don't ask about vacations, coffee breaks, lunch periods, or other details unless or until the job is in fact offered to you. Then you may inquire about them casually before making your own decision, but guard against giving the impression that these things are of paramount importance to you.

14. Never be inquisitive about papers on the interviewer's desk. This is rude in the extreme and gives the interviewer a very poor impression of you.

15. No matter how rude or curt the interviewer may be with you, never respond in kind. Be polite, maintain your poise, and show that you can get along with even disagreeable people.

16. Be careful not to miss the interview-is-over cues. If the interviewer absentmindedly starts to collect his papers or looks at his watch, you have overstayed your welcome. This is an unfortunate and usually unintentional breach of good manners. Before this happens, thank the interviewer for his patience and courtesy and then at once take your leave. Don't linger on and talk yourself out of a job. A graceful exit at the right moment may do more to help you than another half-hour of talk.

17. If the interview is inconclusive you may follow it up with additional information by letter, additional references and explanations. Such a letter, arriving when the employer is considering several applicants, may influence him in your favor. Don't telephone or try to high-pressure the company. Keep your dignity. Don't beg for the job.

DRESSING FOR THE BUSINESS INTERVIEW

This is one of those Very Important Occasions which may change the rest of your life. You may have spent years of study or work to prepare yourself for a job, but they are not going to show immediately when you present yourself for an interview. Your hoped-for employer is going to see your costume, your grooming, your personality as the "outside you" exhibits it. An employer does not want to spend time correcting faults of physical appearance. He is likely to believe that there is a definite relationship between neatness in clothes and that of your file, tools, or desk.

College men and women are often sloppy and given to fads. The business world is not amused by this. Personnel managers have said that inappropriate dress is one of the chief handicaps of the average college graduate.

The first impression you make is important. Walk erectly and purposefully. Dress conservatively and groom yourself with special care. Experts in personnel management warn against school jewelry and against pens and pencils worn in outside pockets. Fraternity and school jewelry is always out of place at such an interview. A woman should particularly avoid a veil that covers her face, a dressy afternoon dress, too much perfume, chipped nails and run-down heels.

GROOMING

In the horse-and-buggy culture of our grandfathers the term *grooming* needed no explaining. One groomed one's horses—brushed, trimmed, tidied them—accordingly as one valued them. By extension, one did the same thing with one's children and oneself, using soap and water in adequate amounts. Today grooming continues to mean basic body cleanness, neatness, trimness. Fashion does not matter here. However you express your personality, do it regularly, neatly, skillfully, and with deliberation.

Good grooming means clean clothes, well-pressed or carefully not pressed. It means shined or brushed shoes without run-down heels. It means stockings without runs. It means clean shirts for men, clean blouses for women, with no frayed or soiled cuffs or collars.

Probably everyone slips up on body-care procedures from time to time. A glance at the following checklist may serve as a useful reminder:

HAIR—Keep the hair on your head clean and orderly. Men should, of course, shave as frequently as necessary. Women should remove heavy growths of hair on the face, legs, hands, or arms. Underarm hair should be removed when sleeveless garments are worn. Always be cautious in removing hair. Shaving is safe but many depilatories have been challenged as to safety.

NAILS—Like hair, your fingernails and toenails keep right on growing no matter how busy you are, and they will not tolerate neglect. Keeping fingernails trimmed to the shape of the finger and toenails cut straight across is probably the least time-consuming method. If women prefer longer, shaped nails, they must allot time to keeping them this way. Nail scissors and nail clippers are quite all right to use but must nearly always be followed by the use of a file or emery stick for smoothing. Jagged nails will catch and tear clothing and are themselves easily broken and torn. Women should use nail lacquers as they use face make-up—to supplement and *not* to cover.

PERSPIRATION AND BODY ODORS—These are caused by the excretion of waste products through the skin and are seldom pleasant. Frequent bathing (and nothing else) will control this problem as far as most of the body is concerned. You do not need special soaps, although most of them do no harm and are pleasant. To control underarm perspiration, especially in women, requires more than daily washing. Use deodorants and antiperspirants as you need them, but make sure you are not allergic to any of their contents. Women should keep dress shields handy for emergencies.

GETTING ALONG IN YOUR JOB

Once the interview is over and you have the job, your next objective is to succeed in it. Like family relationships, job relationships are frequently close and very personal. Seemingly small personality quirks, annoying habits or mannerisms assume disproportionate importance to one's fellow workers and superiors. If things are not going just right—or even if they are—it pays to check oneself against the following behavior reminders occasionally. Be objective, and be honest, in answering these questions:

1. Are you a comfortable person to be with, or do people appear strained in your presence?

2. Do you ruffle easily, or can you maintain a relaxed, easygoing manner in most situations?

3. Are you egotistical? Condescending? Do you enjoy giving the impression that you are the final authority?

4. Do you cultivate the quality of being interesting? Have you something of value to give other people in their association with you?

5. Do you genuinely like other people? If not, do you practice liking them in the effort to acquire this characteristic?

6. Are you alert to every opportunity to congratulate another worker on some achievement? Are you equally sensitive to your co-workers' disappointments and generous in your expressions of sympathy?

7. Do you talk shop with your friends, or in public, and betray your employer's business secrets?

8. If you ask for a raise do you accept the decision quietly and politely, even if the decision is negative? Do you always remember that you must be prepared to leave your job unless you are willing to accept such a decision without rancor?

9. Do you discuss your grievances with your co-workers, oblivious to the fact that you are creating discontent groups among them?

10. Do you ever shift the blame for some mistake onto someone else's shoulders—in other words, pass the buck?

11. Do you sometimes fail to resist the temptation to brag about the relative advantages of your job, your personal or social life?

12. Are you in the habit of taking suggestions, complaints, or information over the head of your immediate superior? (In the case of a serious complaint involving your superior or a situation in which the good of the company is involved, this is of course acceptable procedure, but such instances are rare.)

13. Do you sometimes allow impersonal discussion to degenerate into emotional argument and bickering—a sure basis for disharmony?

14. Do you admit your own mistakes readily and courteously, knowing that a good employer will not tolerate alibis?

15. Do you carry out your assignments with good grace, whether or not you consider them an imposition (knowing that your first responsibility is to get the work out, and that your personal problems will receive more consideration if your work record and personal adjustment is good)?

16. Do you abide by the company policy with regard to smoking, chewing gum, or eating in offices or on the job? If smoking is permitted, do you observe the smoking manners suggested in this book on page 60? *Don't* work or greet someone with a cigarette hanging from your mouth—*don't* smoke in the office of a person who dislikes smoking—*do* empty ash trays often and be neat in your smoking habits. If you are a gum-chewer or are in the habit of eating while working, do you confine these habits to the periods when you are alone and not in contact with the public or co-workers who may find them disturbing? If you chew gum, do you always remember to do it quietly and *with your mouth closed?*

17. Are you in the habit of sponging cigarettes, gum, pencils, or, even worse, money for phone calls, cokes, or coffee?

18. Are you in the habit of taking unauthorized coffee breaks on company time?

19. If you lunch with co-workers (men or women), do you always pick up your own check? (If a man asks a subordinate to lunch

with him for business reasons, he, of course, picks up the check, regardless of whether the subordinate is a man or a woman. In this situation the relationships are those of any social-dining occasion and the people involved will observe all the expected courtesies.)

20. Do you sometimes mistake brusque behavior for businesslike behavior, forgetting that "thank you," "please," "good morning," and other courtesies are at least as important in the work environment as in the social environment?

21. If you have been dismissed, demoted, or passed over for promotion in your company, have you checked your social attitudes and personal adjustments as the possible reason for your problem?

A Man's Manners in Business

It is at least as desirable from a business as from a social point of view that every man should know and practice the accepted manners of his time. The man who ignores the social courtesies is setting up roadblocks to delay or stop his own advancement. The genius' social handicaps might be overlooked (if he is recognized as a genius), but for the average person in business, mannerly attitudes so thoroughly learned as to appear innate are a great advantage. If you find your friends and associates apologizing for your behavior, you are on dangerous ground and should overhaul your social deportment.

Appearance. A man's appearance is more important in public relations jobs than in back-room jobs, but it is always important to the people who have to work in close contact with him. In office jobs, firms vary in their policy on coats, shirts, ties, etc. Some quite rigidly insist on correctness at all times; some are quite indifferent so long as cleanliness and neatness are maintained. In non-air-conditioned offices coats are frequently laid aside during the hot weather, but even in this situation they are put on again for seeing visitors, for leaving the office, or when attending conferences. The chairman of the conference may, however, suggest that coats be removed. In any event, it is well for a new employee to determine the company policy on dress, and then abide by it.

Introductions and names. The etiquette of making introductions and the proper use of names have been discussed in Chapters 2 and 11. Company policies on the use of first names differ. The new employee should take his cue from responsible co-workers or older employees, particularly in regard to the women with whom he works.

When does a man in business rise? In business a man does not rise when his secretary or typist or other woman employee enters his office for business purposes—unless he is greeting her for the first time. He rises when he has a woman caller. Should he be on the telephone at this time, he simply nods and indicates a chair. He may rise if a woman executive enters the room, but only if this will not disrupt business activities and if her status clearly entitles her to special consideration.

In leaving or entering a room a man steps aside to allow his superior to go first, and, regardless of job, the man in business as well as in social life steps aside to allow the woman to precede him through a door.

The businessman—secretary relationship. This will proceed most smoothly if the businessman observes the following reminders:

1. Remember that your secretary is a person and not a machine. She has a private life, private plans, and private interests, which do not necessarily coincide with yours.

2. Your secretary will not expect drawing-room courtesies in the office, but the normal civilities of "please" and "thank you" will expedite your work.

3. Do not ask your secretary to use her free time or lunch hour to do your personal errands. Do not expect her to work late because she has had to take an hour out of her work-time to perform some personal service for you.

4. Don't assume that your secretary is always happy to work overtime. Remember that she may have her own appointments and schedule to meet.

5. Don't expect your secretary to change her plans according to your passing whims. Give her time to make her own plans, and when you have accepted them, abide by them.

FOR WOMEN IN BUSINESS

As we suggested in the early part of this chapter, women have many business relationships whether they are housewives or jobholders. In either situation they function most effectively and most smoothly if they are socially at ease, well-groomed, well-spoken (having a pleasant voice and speaking manner), and alert to the pitfalls that await the unwary woman who uses her femininity as a business prop.

In business, you remember, money-profit is the object, and men tend to be very businesslike about this. So, also, do women when they are in controlling positions. In business you become a partner in a team and winning the objective is the primary interest. Your fellow workers and your bosses like to have attractive, pleasant people on their team, but they don't want distracting influences. It is useful for the woman jobholder to be reminded of a few mistakes that women are inclined to make:

1. Don't overdress, and don't be careless in your dress. According to some authorities, a woman's appearance is rated as high as 75 per cent of her total value when she applies for a job. Employers are often conservative and wish their offices to have a dignified atmosphere. They also assume that a woman who is neat in appearance and person will be neat in her work.

Run-down heels, excessive make-up, exaggerated style of dress, safety-pins replacing buttons, strong perfume, conspicuous colors and fabrics, tight-fitting sweaters or dresses, scanty covering—all of these will count against your promotion and may count against your retaining your job. Particularly in the business situation, simplicity rather than high style is to be emphasized.

After making certain that you are not committing gross errors in your appearance, try to forget the whole thing! This is not easy to do when so much seems to be at stake. However, you *can* learn to resist the temptation to primp all the time. And you *can* learn to appear unself-conscious to other people.

2. Try to be impersonal in your job relationships. Women seem to find it especially hard to accept criticism of their work. Have an adult attitude toward this and remember that it is your *work* and not you, yourself, that is being criticized. Be a pleasant, poised worker,

keeping emotional reactions out of your work. Tears, anger, and jealousies are taboo.

3. Remember that the boss's first responsibility is to his work and the company. If he seems to ignore you and is given to unexplained silences or annoying habits, these are not personal affronts to you. This is a business situation.

4. Keep your private affairs private—and allow your co-workers, your superiors or subordinates to do the same. Don't pry, don't gossip. Be friendly but decline to take part in "gab" sessions on company time.

5. Be honest with the company about your absences and illnesses. You would not take money from the payroll, with which you may be entrusted. Be no less honest about the company's time which is also "entrusted" to you.

THE SECRETARY OR RECEPTIONIST

Since so many women are employed as secretaries or receptionists in business, the following list of procedures and attitudes is suggested for their guidance. In part or in full, it is applicable to nearly all clerical workers and has many worthwhile suggestions for other women jobholders.

1. You represent your firm. Very often you are the first person a visitor sees, your voice is the first voice he hears. A cordial attitude on your part may influence this person toward good relations with your company. A negative attitude on your part may have the opposite effect. Be courteous, poised, tactful, and display the good judgment and intelligence for which you have been hired.

2. Greet callers with "Good morning" or "How do you do?" Do not say "Hello." Do not look up from your work with an annoyed "Yes?" Try to member the names of regular callers. This pleases people, but do not risk a mistake here. It is better to repeatedly ask a person his name than to call him Mr. White if he is Mr. Green.

3. If your desk is located near the door, you do not need to rise to greet callers. If you are located across the room, however, and must raise your voice to be heard, it is better to rise and approach the caller in order to greet him courteously.

4. Greet the visitor promptly. Do not keep him waiting while you finish writing out a sentence. Ask him, "May I help you?"

5. Get the visitor's name and the purpose of his call. If this is something you can properly handle without disturbing your employer, do so, showing genuine interest in his request.

6. If the business in hand is something about which your employer must be consulted, ask the visitor to "Please sit down and I will speak to Mr. King about this."

7. Mr. King may give you some additional information and ask you to conclude whatever business problem the visitor has brought up, or he may wish to see the visitor himself. In this case, you show the visitor into the employer's office and say, "This is Mr. Visitor," or just announce "Mr. Visitor."

8. Later, when the visitor leaves, say, "Good-bye, Mr. Visitor."

9. A visitor who makes an office call rarely objects to telling the purpose of his call, but once in a while some such person will insist on talking only to "the boss." Usually your employer will have given you a directive on this situation, and he will probably have told you under no circumstances to admit such a caller to his office. If, therefore, the visitor hesitates to tell you his business, you may reassure him by saying, "I am Mr. King's secretary, and I will be glad to see Mr. King about an appointment for you when I can tell him what you wish to speak to him about." If the visitor still objects to telling you, suggest that he may prefer to write a letter to Mr. King outlining his problem, and that Mr. King will then decide the appointment hour. Be firm in dealing with such a person but always be polite. Indicate by your voice and manner that the issue is settled, but never be brusque or abusive.

10. Never interrupt your employer unnecessarily. If it is necessary to enter his private office, do so quietly and unobtrusively, without knocking. If he is in conference and you *must* ask him a question, wait for a break in the conversation and then say, "Excuse me, Mr. King, but Mrs. Customer is waiting.. . ." If you have an urgent message for him, write it on a piece of notepaper, slip into the office quietly, and lay the note in front of him.

11. Do not argue with your employer about the "right" way of doing things—no matter what you have learned in your business course in school. While you are working for this employer, his way *is* the right way. You may suggest an alternate way of doing things, but always do the job the way he wants it done. Don't try to remake the boss or the office.

12. Never open your employer's personal mail. If in doubt about a letter, don't open it.

13. When an employer receives a personal telephone call, the tactful secretary leaves the room for its duration.

14. Guard against getting the reputation of being a clock-watcher. You are expected to organize your work so that you can leave promptly when the business day is over. Do not leave unfinished business on your desk, however. Finish what you are doing, and if necessary to stay late, do this cheerfully.

15. If your employer is still at his desk at quitting time, ask him if he needs you before you close up your desk.

16. It is sometimes necessary for secretaries or assistants to travel with male executives. Arrangements for this must always be made in advance. This is done in the firm's name. A hotel will routinely assign accommodations to Mr. Executive and Miss Secretary on separate floors. Mr. Executive registers at the hotel and gives his firm's address rather than his home address, and his secretary follows the same procedure.

THE WIFE'S ROLE IN BUSINESS

Over a period of many years, both business and industry have come to realize their employees' lives cannot be strictly compartmentalized into business affairs and personal affairs. A man's family has a direct and vital interest in the business affairs of its chief breadwinner—usually the husband and father. The breadwinner, similarly, cannot always lay aside personal problems during business hours. His work efficiency may be directly affected by his family relationships. Therefore, business and industry have accepted, and aided in effecting, numerous work, health, life, and retirement insurance measures, the ultimate object being to obtain greater efficiency from their employees.

Following this interest a step further, and in line with the heavy emphasis on psychological influences that has permeated the business world in the last few decades, a number of large corporations have pinpointed the wives of their executives for attention only a little less concentrated than that given to the executives themselves. Wives were interviewed before their husbands were hired, and if they did not pass the test of what a good corporation wife should be like, the husband was very likely not to get the job.

Americans are given to pursuing their "improvement ideas" to extremes for a time and then becoming more sensible, and the "corporation wife" is now seen in more reasonable perspective. Everyone agrees that a man's wife can help or hinder his business career, and this is just as true of the stock clerk as it is of the first vice president in charge of stock.

Organizations whose employees enjoy some social relationships seem to function more smoothly and with less personnel turnover than organizations entirely indifferent to employee outside interests. Wives who can further such relationships are helpful to their husbands and to the organization. What are some of the traits that a wife might usefully cultivate or avoid in her effort to help her husband's career?

1. She should try to keep moderately informed about her husband's work, but she should not pry into business details. These are often confidential in character and her husband is not free to discuss them.

2. If she is on familiar terms with the wives of her husband's co-workers, she should not indulge in company gossip with them.

3. She should not use her husband's position for her own social up-grading, nor should she be obvious in using her own social talents in the effort to push her husband up the success ladder.

4. She should not visit her husband at work unless this is really necessary. There is little objection in most offices, however, if she meets him occasionally at his place of work at the close of the business day.

5. She should be able to entertain her husband's business friends and contacts when necessary and to do this skillfully, graciously, and with tact.

6. She should try to be a good conversationalist and a good listener. It can be helpful to her and to her husband if she likes to read and to keep informed about current events. She should not assume false intellectual (or social) pretensions, but neither should she make a virtue of ignorance.

7. She should dress attractively but she should avoid making others uncomfortable by appearing too chic.

8. She should cultivate poise in the face of unexpected and disconcerting incidents. The ability to handle and get along with people is an invaluable trait in any woman and it is particularly helpful to husbands in business.

THE TELEPHONE IN BUSINESS

Telephone manners have been discussed in this book in some detail in the chapter on conversation. A few comments on the use of the telephone in business may be added here.

A secretary should never give the impression over the telephone that her employer is too busy to be called, but she must use discretion in screening calls. She politely says, "May I ask who is calling?" with an explanation that Mr. Executive is in conference, or in a meeting, or is out of the office, or is simply not available at the moment, or has asked to be interrupted only in an emergency. She then says, "May I give him a message?"

Usually the caller under these circumstances gives his name and volunteers his business. The secretary then promises to turn the matter over to her employer. If the caller objects to telling the secretary his reason for calling, she must firmly and politely insist that "I am sorry but I am unable to reach him now" and conclude the conversation.

The efficient worker in business will plan his or her telephone calls before lifting the receiver. Have the facts on a pad beside the phone. Have any business records you are likely to need within easy reach. These suggestions are particularly important when long distance calls are being made but are good advice for any call. Make your calls as brief as possible. Chatty talk is out of place. Avoid slang —"nope" and "yah." Take time to be polite. Address people by their names and titles. Say, "Yes, Mr. Smith," or "Yes, Sir," and "thank you." Do not say, "Yeah, sure, and thanks."

When you transfer a call to another line, make sure the caller being transferred understands what is going on, and then do not drop the call until you are sure the new contact has been made.

See ye not, Courtesy
Is the true Alchemy,
Turning to gold all it touches
and tries?

—Meredith

15

Travel Tips and Tipping

The cardinal rule for good manners at home and away is consideration for others—courtesy. Good manners are the same in principle everywhere. It seems surprising, then, that our traveling manners are often so bad. Not only is criticism directed against us personally if we are rude, but our friends, our university or school, our country, are all judged accordingly. This means that our travels do not concern only ourselves. They concern everyone with whom we are associated.

The State Department in Washington is very concerned with the manners of traveling Americans. Americans are no longer loved in foreign lands as they were once loved, and our careless habits and poor manners are one reason for this. Every citizen who travels abroad is a United States ambassador, whether he likes being so or not. What you do on your tour of France, Italy, Germany, Japan or any other country will affect your own future and the history of your country and the world. Travel with an open mind. Do not criticize another country because its customs differ from the ones to which you are accustomed. Rather, accept and enjoy the differences. Try to get some background knowledge concerning the country you are visiting. This will add to your enjoyment and understanding. It's their country. Let's remember that.

It is well to remember, too, that traveling within our own country requires the same courteous tolerance that travel abroad requires, and the effects of rudeness here may be more immediate, more personal, and more painful than in travel abroad.

Why We Travel

We do not have to travel. We can always stay at home. Unless traveling is involved in our business, unless we are in some branch of the military service, we travel because we *want* to travel and for no other reason. Why people want to travel is a question that occupies philosophers and psychologists as well as passport and visa officers. Man in his early history was largely nomadic. Why he ever *stopped* traveling is a question that occupies anthropologists, geographers, and historians. According to Nathaniel Hawthorne, "it is so natural for mankind to be nomadic, that a very little taste of that primitive mode of existence subverts the settled habits of many preceding years."

In the twentieth century we live in an age of travel as surely as we live in the age of plastics or the age of the atom. We seem to travel compulsively—that is, when our weeks or months of annual vacation from work or school fall due, we take to the road in one fashion or another almost inevitably. It hardly occurs to us that we have a choice. However, people who travel compulsively may get very little pleasure or benefit from their travels (other than a suntan, and this they can acquire with a little diligence in their own back yards or in city parks or on city rooftops). Travel pleasures and benefits, like other pleasures, benefits, or pains, are experienced mentally. We have often been told that travel is educational, broadening; yet all of us know much-traveled people who are extremely narrow in outlook. "Foreign travel," said a writer of a century ago, "ought to soften prejudices, religious or political, and liberalize a man's mind; but how many there are who seem to have traveled for the purpose of getting up their rancour against all that is opposed to their notions."

Some General Dos and Don'ts for Travelers

1. DON'T go to a foreign country (or any other place) if you particularly dislike that country. You are almost certain to be rude in this situation.

2. DO comply with the manners and customs of the places you visit. For instance, in some countries the wearing of shorts or slacks by women, or the wearing of brief bathing suits, is frowned upon. Remember that you are in a guest situation here. Be careful not to offend the host-country.

3. DON'T be a back-slapper. Don't talk loudly to impress other people, order waiters around, criticize unjustly. In other words, don't be a boor!

4. DON'T gather souvenirs from hotels, trains, or restaurants. What looks like souvenir-collecting to you may look like theft to a hotel owner.

5. DON'T make uncomplimentary remarks in English to your fellow travelers under the impression that the natives will not understand you. This is extremely rude in itself, and, in addition, English is widely understood in many other countries.

6. DO keep your casual-acquaintance relationships impersonal on long trips. Talk with your seat mate or table mate if he or she is interested in talking, but avoid personalities. Names need not be exchanged in this situation, although there is no objection to such an exchange if both parties desire it.

7. DON'T allow casual travel acquaintances to pay for your meals, taxi fares, hotel, or entertainment. This is a must for women and is good advice for men, as well, who may find themselves under embarrassing obligation to a comparative stranger. A courteous "I'll take care of it, thank you" will usually handle this situation.

8. DO be friendly, but avoid over-doing it. Respect your traveling companions' preferences for reading or sleep and try not to interrupt them.

9. DON'T forget to write thank-you notes to friends and family who remembered you with gift, party, or by coming to the airport, station, or dock to see you off. Once out of sight of familiar people and places it is very easy to let familiar duties slip by unful-

filled. It is just as rude to neglect thank-you notes in a travel situation as in the more routine gift [1] situations of our daily lives.

10. DO, if you are responsible for children, try to keep them occupied, happy, and reasonably quiet. Take advantage of every opportunity to let them run about at prolonged station stops. Avoid letting them run through the aisles, climb on seats, or annoy other passengers. Have a good supply of books, crayons, games.

11. DO carry a minimum of luggage. This is good advice no matter what your means of travel will be. Too much luggage can spoil any trip. Experienced travelers travel light. They concentrate on having comfortable, sturdy shoes for the great amount of walking they will inevitably do and on a basic wardrobe keyed to one background color and having durability and ease of care as paramount considerations.

12. DO be neat and clean and help to keep your surroundings neat and clean. Be particularly careful in the washrooms of train or plane. Throw used towels in the containers provided for them. Try not to spill water on the floor. Women should be particularly careful not to leave powder or hair in wash bowls. Clean the bowl with your towel before disposing of it, if necessary.

HOTELS

Unless we are camping-out, or visiting friends or relatives, travel involves us in overnight or longer stop-offs—that is, it involves us in the social situation of becoming paying guests in a hotel, motel, or some other kind of accommodation. If we are well-informed in the techniques and courtesies of the public situations discussed elsewhere in this book, we should not find any serious problems in the hotel

---

[1] Persons giving bon voyage gifts should be very careful to make these suitable. Never give a last-minute gift to an air-traveler; plane-travel luggage is so limited that even an extra pair of nylon stockings can be an embarrassment. Never give bulky gifts for any kind of travel. Luggage for bus travel is also very limited; that for train travel somewhat less so; and for travel by boat it is the least limited, but suitability raises many difficulties. For instance, fruit and candy may go to waste on board a ship where the meals are excellent, elaborate, and plentiful. Inexpensive books that can be passed on to other travelers are welcome gifts. So, also, for some travelers, is wine. Friends may arrange with the steamship company to have this presented at a certain meal.

situation. A few suggestions, however, can further the feeling of familiarity among people not experienced in this area.

1. If possible, make your hotel reservations far enough in advance of your visit for the hotel to confirm your reservation. Avoid misunderstanding and disappointment by making your wishes clear as to single or double room, with or without bath, double or twin beds, and price room you prefer. State a particular location if you consider this necessary. Also give probable length of stay, mentioning days and dates, and the approximate time of arrival.

2. When you arrive at the hotel you will be asked to register—or sign in—at the desk. A man registers as

John Alden, New York (not Mr. John Alden)

A woman registers as

Mrs. John Alden, New York
or
Miss Nancy Alden, New York

Husband and wife register as

Mr. and Mrs. John Alden, New York (not as John Alden and wife)

Husband, wife, and children register as

Mr. and Mrs. John Alden and children, New York
or
. Mr. and Mrs. John Alden, New York
Robert and Nancy
(if children are old enough to receive telephone calls)

3. Hotels provide a number of special services you may wish to take advantage of. For these, use the telephone in your room to call—

Room service, if you wish a meal served in your room. There will be an extra charge for this, as well as the usual tip for the waiter who serves you.

Bar service for drinks.

Housekeeper for extra blankets.

You may also ask the desk (the voice at the other end of your room telephone) to rouse you at some specified hour in the morning. They will do this by means of your telephone.

4. When your visit is over and you are ready to leave the hotel, call the desk, say you are checking out, and ask for a bellboy to carry your luggage. Or, if you are a man and are traveling very light, you will probably carry your own bag down to the desk, where you will pay your bill and turn over your room key (unless you have left your room key in the room—a very usual procedure).

If you are checking out of a hotel in Europe, it is advisable to call the desk several hours in advance of your departure, or even the night before, to give the management time to prepare the complicated bill.

5. The term *European plan* hotel refers to the typical city hotel with room and meals priced separately.

If the hotel is operated on the *American plan* (as are many resort hotels), the price stated usually includes two meals and room.

TRAIN TRAVEL

Make your reservations in advance for any train travel other than "no reserved seats" coach travel. Accommodations range in this order of cost: regular coach, reserved-seat coach, reserved Pullman chair, upper berth, lower berth, roomette, bedroom, compartment (1–3 people), drawing room (1–4 people). The final four in this list have private toilet facilities.

When traveling in a day coach you are expected to handle your own luggage. When traveling Pullman a man may handle his own luggage, but a woman usually gives her car and seat number to a porter, who then finds the seat and stows her luggage for her. The car porter will also stow luggage and will take care of passenger needs during the trip—pillows, card tables, refreshments. You are expected to push the bell button near your seat to call the porter.

Be careful that your luggage does not protrude into the aisle, as someone may trip over it and fall. This is particularly likely to happen in a day coach.

If you are traveling alone and are occupying a double seat, it is considerate of you to exchange your seat with a husband and wife or adult and child who cannot find seats together. If there is any shortage of seats in your car, it is *in*considerate of you to monopolize the vacant seat beside you or across from you with your possessions.

Do not linger in the dining car when there are other people waiting to be served. Although you may speak to an unknown person at your table in the diner, it is not rude if you prefer to read.

Americans, accustomed to going to the dining car when they are hungry, should realize that when traveling in Europe, they must make prior reservations for a first, second, or third seating before they will be allowed to enter the diner.

If your trip is an overnight one and your reservation is anything other than a berth, you can go to bed at any time simply by entering your room and closing the door. If your reservation is for a berth, it will be necessary for the porter to make up the beds before you can retire. It is courteous for you to consult your seat companion before ringing for the porter for this purpose, since the seats cannot be used after the berths are made up. Probably ten o'clock, or ten-thirty, is a reasonable hour for retiring, although this depends greatly on the length of your trip. Many people go to bed much earlier than this and those who wish to stay up late generally do so in the observation or club car.

The person occupying the upper berth is expected to ring for the porter when getting into and out of the bed. The porter will provide a small ladder to make this process easy and safe.

Berth occupants may dress and undress either in the narrow confines of their beds or in the car dressing rooms. Since the latter are often crowded, especially in the early morning, it is often most convenient to partially dress in the berth and complete the process in the dressing room.

The person who has paid for the lower berth in a section expects to ride during the day in the forward-facing seat. However, this is a right few courteous people would insist upon if the upper-berth companion found riding backwards uncomfortable. Nor would they often insist upon it if the upper-berth companion simply pre-empted the seat—ignorantly or intentionally. Pleasurable travel demands tolerance and a willingness to shrug off distasteful occurrences.

Many of the above suggestions for travel by Pullman car hold good for travel by coach in the reserved reclining-seat accommodations. Under these circumstances, of course, passengers do not actually go to bed at night, but the porter will supply pillows at a small charge and many people find the half-reclining seat position quite tolerable for a one-night trip or even a longer trip. Since privacy is impossible in this travel situation, it is particularly important for all persons to be neat, polite, and above all considerate of their fellow passengers. Seat-holders in these cars are entitled to the use of the dining cars and lounge cars in exactly the same way as are the Pullman travelers.

PLANE TRAVEL

Reservations for travel by air should be made whenever possible well in advance of flight, and they should be confirmed before going to the airport. Seats on domestic flights are usually not reserved but are selected according to your preference as you enter the plane. This is not a hard-and-fast rule, however, and may vary with the flight and with the line. Seats on intercontinental flights usually are reserved in advance. Although all seats are comfortable, the ride may be a little rougher near the tail. Seats over the wing have a restricted view but some people prefer these seats in spite of this fact. A plane traveler who has entered and claimed a seat may use an "Occupied" sign to hold the seat if he wishes to leave the plane temporarily.

Good plane manners are essentially the same as good train manners. Such special problems as arise are likely to be strictly regulated by the air lines. The stewardess is the arbiter of manners in the air, and the passenger who conforms with her suggestions is likely to find the trip pleasant. The fact that special conditions alter customs is amusingly illustrated by the button-under-the-chin napkin that is sometimes presented for your use at meals. Etiquette very much approves of this compromise. Remember to thank the stewardess for her trouble in your behalf when you leave the plane. Her status is that of a professional and offering her a tip would be in very bad form.

TRAVEL BY SHIP

In addition to the amenities and manners suitable to travel in general, travel by ship involves some special behavior and formalities which we consider briefly here.

Embarking for an international voyage can be a prolonged process. Plan to arrive at the pier at least an hour before sailing time for this purpose.

As soon as you are free to do so, seek out the dining steward and make a table and first- or second-seating reservation for your meals. People with small children are expected to eat at the first seating. Then go to the deck steward to reserve your steamer chair. You will have a better chance of getting the location and time you prefer if you do these things promptly. If you have made your reservations through a travel agent, you will probably find that your table and deck chair arrangements have been taken care of. However, it is wise to confirm the arrangements. Unless you have a private bath, you must also schedule your bath time with the bath steward.

On board ship you naturally introduce yourself at the dining table and to those who sit near you in your deck chair. People sit at the Captain's table by invitation only, and being invited to do so is thought to be an honor. If you should receive this invitation, be prompt and observe the usual guest-host amenities. The Captain's guests do not leave his table until the Captain does so.

Since the cabins of most ships are likely to be small and crowded places, it is very important for your own comfort that you keep your belongings in order. If you share the cabin with a stranger this becomes doubly important.

The clothing you will wear on shipboard will be similar to resort wear. In general, conservative sport clothes are good for daytime wear. Shorts and bathing suits are suitable for wear in the sports and swimming areas. Men wear coats to all meals. Except in the tourist and cabin class, and depending upon the size of the ship, there is some attempt at evening formality. Even this is usually optional, however. On the first and last nights out very few people attempt to dress for dinner as clothing is usually packed away at this time.

TRAVEL BY PRIVATE CAR OR BUS

In traveling by whatever means on the public highway you will be involved in the social situations we have previously discussed as associated with hotel (motel, tourist rooms, etc.), restaurant, and public situations in general. Awareness of the manners suitable to

these situations should carry you through most highway relationships. If you are traveling as one of a group in a private car, you will
be wise to make definite arrangements about sharing expenses before
starting out. Also, take care to load the car with no more than your
share of luggage.

TIPPING

HOW MUCH AND WHEN?

Tipping is one of the universal problems of etiquette. People
who are at ease in most social situations are often confused by the
problems of when, how, and how much to give. Tipping is thought
by many to be an undesirable and undignified system. In principle
they are right, but since this system does happen to be in force, one
should probably pay his share for services rendered. The tipping system is expected to make up the difference between base pay and a
living wage; it is even more widely used in other countries than in
the United States.

Although there is no law which forces you to tip, you may be
criticized if you fail to tip or are niggardly with amounts; you will
also be criticized if you bestow your tips too extravagantly, or in an
ostentatious manner.

If the service has been slow, discourteous, inadequate, you need
not feel self-conscious about not tipping, but be very sure you penal-
ize the offending person. The slow service may be due to the kitchen
help rather than to the waitress whom you decide not to tip.

On the other hand, extra tips should be left for extra service—
help with children, patience on the part of the waitress when you
linger during rush hours, any extra demands.

"Thank you very much," a smile, and "Everything has been
very pleasant" is always appreciated by service employees.

WHOM SHOULDN'T YOU TIP?

1. The owner, proprietor, or manager of an establishment, such
as a banker, or the owner-operator of the beauty shop or barber
shop.

2. Professionals, such as nurse, companion, or governess. A gift
may be given but not money.

3. Do not tip where there are signs saying, "No Tipping."
4. Do not tip on top of paying a service charge. In this situation, salaries are adequate or are made so when the service charge has been added to the bill. A tip is as embarrassing to the employee who should refuse it as to the person whose gratuity is refused. It is permissible to ask if in doubt.

5. An employee in a private club by members or guests (in private country clubs the "No Tipping" rule is now often relaxed).

Don't be trapped. Often those who expect tips play on people's uncertainty or embarrassment about tips in order to get more than the fair amount. A cab driver may give you two quarters in change after a fifty-cent fare, hoping for a quarter tip. A ladies' room attendant who keeps nothing but quarters or fifty-cent pieces on her silver tray hopes you will think everyone tips that much rather than the usual fifteen cents—even though she has merely handed you a towel. There is no reason to be embarrassed—take time to get the right change and make your tips fair but not excessive. Do not tip after discourteous service.

Make a point of always having a pocketful of change. This will help you to avoid both under-tipping and over-tipping. Ask fellow travelers, if in doubt.

THE TIPPING TABLE

This table is a composite of the conclusions of a large number of experienced travelers. Use it as a rough guide.

TRAIN TRAVEL
Porter (*Redcap*) —$.25 a bag at most terminals when fee is set.
Porter (*train*)   —$.50 to $.75 for a day trip (with Pullman accommodations).
$.75 to $1 for an overnight berth.
$1 or $2 for a roomette or drawing room.
Scale goes down if trip is longer than one night.
Dining-car waiter—15 per cent of cost of meal.
Club-car steward —15 per cent of bill (not less than $.25).

AIR TRAVEL
No tips allowed from time luggage reaches the scales at airport until you get it back at baggage room at point of destination. This rule does not always have the support of the employees and a tip may speed

your baggage through to you. However, tipping under these conditions takes the form of a bribe.

$.25 a bag to *porter* who assists you with your luggage before it is weighed in or after it has been checked out.

TRAVEL BY SHIP

About 10 per cent of the cost of passage should be divided among those who serve you. Approximate amounts are:

Room steward—30 per cent

Table steward—30 per cent

Room stewardess—20 per cent

Bath steward—10 per cent

Deck steward—10 per cent

Bartender—15 per cent of each bill each time you pay.

$.25 to $.50 for *porter* who puts luggage on escalator. At some steamship piers large signs say, "No Tipping."

No tips for purser or officers of ship. Always thank them at end of voyage.

RESTAURANT

Headwaiter—Don't tip unless for special table or when reservation is made in advance. $1 to $5 depending on place. Tipping in advance may assure a good table, although one rarely tips except in American-plan hotels.

Waiter or *waitress*—generally 15 per cent of bill.

Busboy—no tip in most places. Waitress sometimes shares the tip with him and with the kitchen help.

Wine steward—10 per cent of wine bill. Not less than $1, determined by the quality of the restaurant.

Lunch counter—often nothing, or $.05 for coffee to $.15 to $.25 for light meal.

HOTEL

Doorman—nothing for helping you out of door. $.25 for getting cab.

Bellboy—$.25 a bag if he can handle luggage in one trip. $.10 for getting a newspaper and $.25 for delivering package.

Porter or *bell captain*—$.50 for trunk, $.50 to $1 for getting theater tickets or any such service.

Chambermaid—nothing at European-plan hotel unless she does something special. $1 or $2 a week at American-plan hotel. Resident at hotel $1 a month.

Headwaiter—Often nothing. Transient who wants to be sure of a good table about $1. Residents $3 to $5 every few weeks. $1 to $5 for family at resort hotel for each week.

Room waiter—15 per cent of check, $.25 minimum.

Valet—generally nothing unless a rush job is done outside of hours. He operates his own shop.

Page boys—$.10 to $.25 depending on size of hotel. Tip depends on amount of walking he does to reach you.

Elevator man—nothing for short stay. About $1 for long stay. Residents $1 a month.

Hat check girl—$.15 to $.25 depending on type hotel and if a special affair like a dance.

OTHERS

Rest room attendant—$.10 or $.15. For special services $.25.

Barber—$.25.

Beauty operator—$.25 or 10 per cent cost of permanent.

Parking lot attendant—usually nothing. Where expected $.10 a time or $1 or $2 occasionally if regular patron.

Department store doorman—nothing if he merely opens the door. $.25 if he calls a cab.

Cigarette girl—$.10.

Hospital attendants—$1 for 5 or 10 day stay. $3 to $4 for month stay. Never tip a nurse.

Taxi driver—$.15 for a fare up to $.60. 20 per cent for fares above $.60. The tip should be slightly more if it is late at night or if the driver helps with heavy luggage.

On the golf course—Tips vary—safe minimums are: if the fee is under $2.00, tip $.25. If the fee is over $2.00, tip $.50. Do not tip a golf master or pro. Tips are higher in tournaments. Tip the locker room attendant $1.00 in a private club, but less on a public course.

After a Visit at a Private Home

You need not tip the house servants unless you have spent a weekend or more. You don't usually tip a servant you have not seen. Try to give the tip when you say goodbye and not in front of the hostess. Some households have abolished tipping.

Tips amount to $1 to $5 per servant.

Women usually don't tip men servants except chauffeur.

Man guest—$1 to *chauffeur*. $1 to $2 to *maid* after an overnight stay. $2 to $5 to *maid* after a week's stay.

Woman guest—$1 to $2 to *chambermaid* or *waitress* after an overnight stay. $2 to $5 to a *maid* after a weekend stay.

Couple—$2 to $3 to *maid* after an overnight stay. $3 to $5 to *maid* after a weekend stay.

Reading Suggestions

General

AMES, ELINOR, *Etiquette for Moderns* (New York, Walker and Company, 1965).

BEVANS, MARGARET, *McCall's Book of Everyday Etiquette* (New York, Golden Press, 1960).

BRACKEN, PEG, *I Try to Behave Myself* (New York, Harcourt, 1964).

CORINTH, KAY and SARGENT, MARY, *All About Entertaining* (New York, McKay, 1966).

CUMING, LUELLA, *Course in Social Awareness, Poise, and Gracious Living* (Englewood Cliffs, N.J., Prentice-Hall, 1965).

DARIAUX, GENEVIÉVE ANTOINE, *Entertaining with Elegance* (Garden City, N.Y., Doubleday, 1965).

Esquire Magazine, *The New Esquire Etiquette* (Philadelphia, Lippincott, 1959).

FENWICK, MILLICENT, *Vogue Book of Etiquette* (New York, Simon and Schuster, 1948).

POST, EMILY, *Etiquette* (New York, Funk & Wagnalls, 1965).

———, *Meal Time Etiquette* (New York, Pocket, 1963).

RAYMOND, LOUISE, *Good Housekeeping's Book of Today's Etiquette* (New York, Harper, 1965).

ROOSEVELT, ELEANOR, *Book of Common Sense Etiquette* (New York, Macmillan, 1962).

SHAW, CAROLYN HAGNER, *Modern Manners* (New York, Dutton, 1958).

STEPHENSON, MARGARET and MILLET, R. L., *As Others Like You* (New York, McKnight, 1959).

VANDERBILT, AMY, *Complete Book of Etiquette* (Garden City, N.Y., Doubleday, 1958).

———, *Everyday Etiquette* (Garden City, N.Y., Doubleday, 1967).

Business

BECKER, ESTHER R. and LAURENCE, R. L., *Success and Satisfaction in Your Office Job* (New York, Harper, 1954).

JAMES, BARRY, *A Man's Guide to Business and Social Success* (Bronx, N.Y., Milady Publishing, 1966).

———, *Parker Publishing Co.'s Business Etiquette Handbook* (West Nyack, N.Y., Parker Publishing, 1964).

SHEEHAN, R., "Business Manners," *Fortune* (January, 1955).

VERMES, JEAN, *The Secretary's Guide to Dealing with People* (West Nyack, N.Y., Parker Publishing, 1964).

Teen Age

ALLEN, BETTY and BRIGGS, MITCHELL, *Mind Your Manners* (Philadelphia, Lippincott, 1964).

BEERY, MARY, *Manners Made Easy* (New York, McGraw-Hill, 1966).

———, *Young Teens Plan Dates and Proms* (New York, McGraw-Hill, 1962).

———, *Young Teens Away From Home* (New York, McGraw-Hill, 1966).

CLARK, MARY ELIZABETH and QUIGLEY, M. C., *Etiquette Jr.* (Garden City, N.Y., Doubleday, 1965).

CROUNAE, HELEN LOUISE, *Joyce Jackson's Guide to Dating* (Englewood Cliffs, N.J., Prentice-Hall, 1957).

HAUPT, ENID A., *Seventeen Book of Etiquette and Entertaining* (New York, McKay, 1963).

——, *Seventeen Guide to Your Widening World* (New York, Macmillan, 1965).

LEAF, MUNRO, *Manners Can Be Fun* (Philadelphia, Lippincott, 1958).

PIERSON, IRENE, *Campus Cues* (Danville, Ill., The Interstate, 1962).

STRATTON, DOROTHY and SCHLEMAN, HELEN, *Your Best Foot Forward* (New York, McGraw-Hill, 1955).

Weddings

BIRMINGHAM, FRANCES and FREDERICK, A., *The Wedding Book* (New York, Harper, 1964.)

Bride's Magazine, *The Bride's Book of Etiquette* (New York, Grosset & Dunlap, 1967).

WILSON, BARBARA, *Bride's School Complete Book of Engagement and Wedding Etiquette* (New York, Hawthorn-McClelland, 1959).

The Armed Forces

JEROME, SALLY and SHEA, N. B., *Marine Corps Wife* (New York, Harper, 1955).

HARRAL, BROOKS, J., SWARTZ, ORETHA D., *Service Etiquette* (Annapolis, Md., United States Naval Institute, 1961).

McEVOY, P., "Good Manners Are Taught at West Point," *Ladies Home Journal* (August, 1966).

SHEA, NANCY BRINTON, *The Air Force Wife* (New York, Harper, 1966).

WIER, ESTER and HICKEY, DOROTHY COFFIN, *The Answer Book on Air Force Social Customs* (Harrisburg, Pa., Military Service Publishing Co., 1957).

———, *Army Social Customs* (Harrisburg, Pa., Military Service Division, Stackpole Co., 1960).

———, *Answer Book on Naval Social Customs* (Harrisburg, Pa., Military Service Publishing Co., 1956).

———, *Washington, D.C. Etiquette and Protocol* (New York, Harcourt, 1956).

Appendix

CORRECT FORMS OF ADDRESS

THE PERSON	INTRODUCTION	CONVERSATION	SALUTATION (LETTER)	CLOSING (LETTER)	ENVELOPE
Clergy and Church Officials Protestant clergyman	Dr. or Mr. Hall Pastor or The Reverend Dr. Hall	Dr. Hall or Mr. Hall	My Dear Dr. Hall or Dear Mr. Hall	Sincerely yours or Very truly yours	The Reverend John Hall or The Reverend John White, D.D.

THE PERSON	INTRODUCTION	CONVERSATION	SALUTATION (LETTER)	CLOSING (LETTER)	ENVELOPE
Episcopal Bishop	Bishop Brown	Bishop Brown	My dear Bishop Brown	Sincerely yours or Faithfully yours	The Right Reverend Robert Brown or The Bishop of Ohio
Methodist Bishop	Bishop Adams	Bishop Adams	My dear Bishop Adams or Dear Sir	Respectfully yours or Sincerely yours	The Reverend James Adams or The Methodist Bishop of Harrisburg
Dean	The Dean of St. Matthews or Dean Smith	Mr. Dean	My dear Mr. Dean or Very Reverend Sir	Respectfully yours or Sincerely yours	The Very Reverend John Smith, D.D. or The Dean of St. Matthews' Cathedral
Rabbi	Rabbi Kahn or Dr. Kahn	Rabbi or Rabbi Kahn	My dear Rabbi Kahn or Sir (business)	Sincerely yours or Very truly yours	Rabbi Joseph Kahn or Dr. Joseph Kahn

The Pope	His Holiness or The Pope or The Pontiff or The Holy Father	Your Holiness or Most Holy Father	Your Holiness or Most Holy Father	Your Holiness' most humble servant	His Holiness, the Pope or His Holiness Pope John
Cardinal	His Eminence or Cardinal Torrent	Your Eminence	Your Eminence	I have the honor to remain or Your Eminence's humble servant	His Eminence Patrick Torrent
Archbishop	The Most Reverend or The Archbishop of Los Angeles	Your Excellency	Your Excellency or Most Reverend Sir	I have the honor to remain with high respect or Respectfully yours or Sincerely yours	The Most Reverend John Doe Archbishop of Los Angeles

THE PERSON	INTRODUCTION	CONVERSATION	SALUTATION (LETTER)	CLOSING (LETTER)	ENVELOPE
Roman Catholic Bishop	Bishop or The Most Reverend	Your Excellency	Your Excellency or My dear Bishop Kelly	Faithfully yours or Sincerely yours	The Right Reverend John Kelly, Bishop of Boston or The Most Reverend
Monsignor	Monsignor Murphy or The Right Reverend Monsignor	Monsignor Murphy	Right Reverend or Dear Monsignor Murphy	Respectfully yours or Sincerely yours	The Right Reverend Monsignor Murphy
Priest	Father Johns or The Reverend Father Johns	Father or Father Johns	Dear Father Johns	Faithfully yours or Sincerely yours	The Reverend Robert Johns or The Reverend Father Robert Johns
Mother Superior	Reverend Mother	Reverend Mother	Reverend Mother or Dear Reverend Mother Mary	Sincerely yours or Yours faithfully	The Reverend Mother Superior or The above plus the initials or name of her order

	Spoken	Salutation	Complimentary close	Envelope
Sister	Sister or Sister Mary	My dear Sister or My dear Sister Mary	Sincerely yours or Yours respectfully	Sister Mary (initials or name of her order)
Brother	Brother Paul	Brother or Brother Paul	Dear Brother or Dear Brother Paul	Yours respectfully or Sincerely yours	The Reverend Brother Paul Sheean (initials or name of his order)
Government Officials * The President	The President or Only the name of person introduced is spoken	Mr. President	My dear Mr. President or Mr. President (business)	Yours faithfully or Yours respectfully or Sincerely yours	The President The White House Washington, D.C.
The Vice President	The Vice President	Mr. Vice President or Sir (occasionally in conversation)	My dear Mr. Vice President	Sincerely yours or Very truly yours (business) or Respectfully yours	The Vice President United States Senate Washington, D.C.

237

* In the United States the courtesy title of The Honorable is given to most high officials of our federal and state governments. They keep this title for the rest of their lives, although they never apply it to themselves. The Honorable should be written in full.

THE PERSON	INTRODUCTION	CONVERSATION	SALUTATION (LETTER)	CLOSING (LETTER)	ENVELOPE
The Chief Justice of the Supreme Court	The Chief Justice or The Honorable Thomas Walker	Mr. Chief Justice	Dear Mr. Chief Justice or Sir (business)	Sincerely Yours or Very truly yours (business)	The Chief Justice The Supreme Court Washington, D.C.
Associate Justice of the Supreme Court	Mr. Justice Downs	Mr. Justice	My dear Mr. Justice or Sir (business)	Sincerely yours or Very truly yours (business)	Mr. Justice Downs or The Honorable John Downs
Member of the President's cabinet	The Secretary of State or The Honorable David Hunt	Mr. Secretary or Madam Secretary	My dear Mr. Secretary or Dear Sir	Sincerely yours or Very truly yours (business)	The Secretary of State Washington, D.C. or The Honorable David Hunt Secretary of State
United States or state Senator	Senator Wood or Senator Wood of New York	Senator Wood or Mr. Senator	Dear Senator Wood or Dear Sir	Sincerely yours or Very truly yours (business)	Senator Richard Wood or The Honorable Richard Wood

United States Representative or state legislator	Mr. Doe	Mr. Doe	Dear Mr. Doe (DO NOT write) Dear Congressman or Dear Representative	Respectfully or Sincerely yours or Very truly yours (business)	The Honorable Mark Doe House of Representatives Washington, D.C. or State Assembly Harrisburg, Pa.
Governor	The Governor or The Governor of Texas or Governor White	Governor or Governor White	Dear Governor White or My dear Governor	Respectfully or Sincerely yours	The Honorable Keith White, Governor of Texas Austin, Texas
Mayor	Mayor Green or The Mayor	Mayor Green or Mr. Mayor	My dear Mayor Green or Dear Sir	Sincerely yours or Very truly yours	The Honorable John Green, Mayor of Seattle, Seattle, Washington

239

THE PERSON	INTRODUCTION	CONVERSATION	SALUTATION (LETTER)	CLOSING (LETTER)	ENVELOPE
Judge	Judge Jones	Judge Jones	My dear Judge Jones	Sincerely yours or Very truly yours (business)	The Honorable John Jones
Ambassador	The Ambassador of Denmark	Mr. Ambassador or Your Excellency	My dear Mr. Ambassador or Your Excellency	Sincerely yours or Very truly yours (business)	His Excellency, The Ambassador of Denmark
American Chargé d'Affaires or consular officer	Mr. White	Mr. White	Dear Mr. White or Dear Sir	Very truly yours or Respectfully or Sincerely yours	John White, Esq. American Consul Paris, France Mr. John White Chargé d'Affaires
Minister (in diplomatic service)	Mr. Minister	Mr. Minister	My dear Mr. Minister	Very truly yours or Respectfully or Sincerely yours	The Honorable Carl Black, Minister of Switzerland

Members of the Armed Services**					
Officer of the Navy with grade of Commander or higher and officer of the Army, Air Force, or Marines with grade of Captain or higher	Admiral Bauer Captain Seabury of the Navy	Admiral Bauer Captain Seabury	Dear Admiral Bauer Dear Captain Seabury or Dear Sir	Very truly yours or Sincerely yours	Admiral Bruce Bauer Captain David Seabury
Junior officer in Navy, Army, Air Force, or Marines	Ensign Durham Lieutenant Runk	Mr. Durham Mr. Runk	Dear Mr. Durham Dear Mr. Runk or Dear Sir	Very truly yours or Sincerely yours	Ensign William Durham 2nd Lieutenant John Runk

** Careful attention should be given to precise rank. If the serviceman is retired, Rtd. is added to his name. Doctors in the service with a rank of Lieutenant and above are addressed by their rank. Junior officers are often called Doctor. Chaplains are always called, socially and officially, Chaplain, no matter what the rank is. A Catholic priest may be called Father.

Noncommissioned officers are addressed by title. Sergeant may be used to address all grades of Sergeants, although socially Mr. may be used.

In the Navy, Commanders, including Lieutenant Commander and above, are addressed socially by their Navy title. All below that rank are Mr., socially. Cadets of the U.S. Military Academy are Mister socially but Cadet officially. National Guard and Reserve officers not on active duty do not use their titles socially or in business affairs, unless their activities have some bearing on military matters. Gentlemen, regardless of rank, are introduced or presented to ladies. This holds even though the gentleman may be distinguished and the lady young. Junior officers should be brought to senior officers for introductions.

THE PERSON	INTRODUCTION	CONVERSATION	SALUTATION (LETTER)	CLOSING (LETTER)	ENVELOPE
Miscellaneous Medical doctor	Dr. Bauer (man) or Dr. Bauer or Mrs. Bauer (woman) (socially)	Doctor or Dr. Bauer	Dear Dr. Bauer	Sincerely yours or Very truly yours (business)	Dr. Lester E. Bauer, Jr. (office or home) Dr. Dianne Bauer (office) or Mrs. Lester E. Bauer, Jr. (home)
Professor or Academic Doctor	Professor Light or Dr. Light or Mr. (Mrs.) Light (socially)	Mr. Light or Dr. Light or Professor Light	Dear Dr. Light or Dear Professor Light	Sincerely yours or Very truly yours	Dr. James Light or Professor James Light or James Light, Ph.D.
Widow	Mrs. Black	Mrs. Black	Dear Mrs. Black	Sincerely yours	Mrs. John Black (same as when her husband was alive)
Divorcée	Mrs. Evans	Mrs. Evans	Dear Mrs. Evans	Sincerely yours	Mrs. Wells Evans (her maiden surname followed by ex-husband's last name)

242

| Married woman who uses her maiden name professionally | Mrs. Blank (socially) or Miss Tiffany (business) | Mrs. Blank (socially) or Miss Tiffany (business) | Dear Mrs. Blank (socially) or Dear Miss Tiffany (business) | Sincerely yours or Very truly yours (business) | Mrs. John Blank (home address) or Miss Jean Tiffany (office address) |

Index